Growing with Music

HARRY R. WILSON

WALTER EHRET

ALICE M. SNYDER

EDWARD J. HERMANN

ALBERT A. RENNA

Illustrated by JOHN MOODIE

BOOK 4

Prentice-Hall, Inc.

Englewood Cliffs, New Jersey

The authors of *Growing with Music* wish to thank the many people who have contributed original material for this book. Every effort has been made to locate owners of other materials and grateful acknowledgment is due the publishers for permission to reprint copyrighted materials.

HARRY R. WILSON, *Chairman of the Music Department*
Teachers College, Columbia University

WALTER EHRET, *Supervisor of Vocal Music*
Scarsdale Schools, Scarsdale, New York

ALICE M. SNYDER, *Associate Professor of Music Education*
San Francisco State College

EDWARD J. HERMANN, *Associate Professor of Music*
Louisiana State University

ALBERT A. RENNA, *Director of Music*
San Francisco Unified School District

As an aid to teaching and interpretation, all songs in "Growing with Music,"
Book 4 are recorded and are available in a boxed set
of eight 12-inch L.P. albums, from Prentice-Hall, Inc.

The music in this book was reproduced from handwritten originals by Maxwell Weaner.

© 1963 by PRENTICE-HALL, INC., Englewood Cliffs, N.J.

Printed in the United States of America

36580–E

Library of Congress Catalog Card Number: 63-7629

Contents

Old folks, young folks,
Children always gay;
Boys and girls a-growing
While singing at their play.
—ANONYMOUS

MOOD IN MUSIC

I'm Gonna Sing

SPIRITUAL

Brightly

1. I'm gon - na sing when the spir - it says, "sing,"

I'm gon - na sing when the spir - it says, "sing,"

I'm gon - na sing when the spir - it says, "sing,"

And o - bey the spir - it of the Lord.

2. I'm gonna shout . . .   3. I'm gonna preach . . .   4. I'm gonna pray . . .

1

The Night is Serene

WORDS ADAPTED BY WILLIAM CLARK
SPANISH FOLK SONG

La noche 'sta serena is Spanish for "the night is serene." What English words can you make up to fit the melody and the mood of this gentle peaceful song?

Peacefully

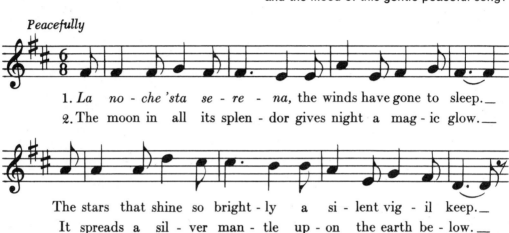

1. *La no - che 'sta se - re - na,* the winds have gone to sleep.
2. The moon in all its splen - dor gives night a mag - ic glow.

The stars that shine so bright - ly a si - lent vig - il keep.
It spreads a sil - ver man - tle up - on the earth be - low.

The gen - tle breez - es hur - ry by and whis - per to the trees,
The night - in - gale breaks in - to song that ech - oes through the air,

They seem to go no cer - tain way but wan - der as they please.
The night so qui - et and se - rene is here for us to share.

Here is a bell part you can play as you sing. It uses only two tones.
In the last four measures, you can complete the bell part by using the same two tones.

Sing Your Way Home

The first note of this song is the third scale tone, **mi.** What is the letter name of the home tone?

TRADITIONAL

Cheerfully

Sing your way home at the close of the day,

Sing your way home, drive the shad - ows a - way.

Smile ev - 'ry mile, for wher - ev - er you roam

It will bright - en your road, It will light - en

your load, If you sing your way home.

The key signature of this song is one sharp. You will understand the key signature better if you look on page 102. The sharp shows that all F's in the song are raised one half step. Two other sharps are used, one before an A and one before a G. These sharps affect only the notes in the measure where they occur. The barline at the end of the measure cancels the sharps. When a sharp or flat that is not in the key signature is used in a song, we call it an **accidental.**
   Sing the melody without the accidentals. You will hear how they add color.

It's a Hap-Hap-Happy Day

WORDS BY AL J. NEIBURG
MUSIC BY SAMMY TIMBERG AND WINSTON SHARPLES

It's a hap-hap-hap-py day, Too-dle, oo-dle, oo-dle,

oo-dle, oo-dle ay. For you and me, for us and we,

All the clouds have roll'd a-way. It's a hap-hap-hap-py day,

Too-dle, oo-dle, oo-dle, oo-dle, oo-dle ay. The sun-shine's

bright and the world's all right, It's a hap-hap-hap-py day.

4

Four and twen - ty sun - beams are danc - ing 'round my face,

Four score and twen - ty more are danc - ing ev - 'ry place.

It's a hap - hap - hap - py day, Too - dle, oo - dle, oo - dle,

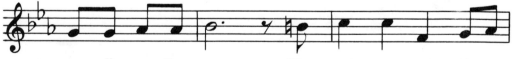

oo - dle, oo - dle ay. You can't go wrong if you

sing a song, It's a hap - hap - hap - py day.

Moon on Ruined Castle

WORDS BY HARRY EVANS
JAPANESE FOLK TUNE

Lift the round flat moon
Snap this twig for handle . . .
What a pretty fan!

—SOKAN

Peacefully

1. Mid the fra - grant flow - ers, nod - ding in the breeze,
Ha - ru ko - o ro - o - no, Ha - na no e - un,

Stand the crum - bling cas - tle walls, lost in mem - o - ries;
Me gu ru - so Ka - zu ki, Ka - ge so shi - te;

In the moon's soft ra - di - ance, phan - tom voic - es, low,
Chi - yo no ma tsu - ga - e, Wa - ke - i - de - shi,

Wake the ghost - ly ech - oes, Of days long a - go.
Mu ka shi no hi - ka - ri, I - ma oi - zu ko.

2. Leaves are painted red and gold, brushed by autumn's sun,
Cold winds whisper to the trees, "Summer days are done."
On the hill a castle stands, black against the sky,
By its walls the rustling leaves gather one by one.

6

Viking Song

WORDS BY MADELEINE A. DUFAY
NORWEGIAN FOLK TUNE

Sturdily

1. Hoist the sail and give three cheers,
Where the mid - night sun ap - pears,

Wide is the sea be - fore us,
Blue are the skies shin - ing o'er us!

Sail - ing, sail - ing to the sea,

Now join the Vik - ing cho - rus!

2. Far beyond the land we sail,
Riding the tide as it's flowing,
On to find the shark and the whale,
Where ocean breezes are blowing,
Sailing, sailing to the sea,
Our Viking ships are going!

7

I'm Singing of Springtime

WORDS BY YVONNE CARR
ENGLISH MELODY

Happily

1. I'm sing-ing _ of spring-time when the birds fly in a blue sky,
2. I'm sing-ing _ of spring-time when the buds grow and the brooks flow,

A song of _ sweet spring - time, feel the breeze through the trees.
A song of _ sweet spring - time of the gay month of May.

Autumn

WORDS BY JOAN LAMSON
MUSIC BY FELIX MENDELSSOHN

Moderately

1. Au - tumn is the time of year When bright leaves are fall - ing,
2. Wheat and corn in gold - en fields Read - y for the reap - ing,

Lis - ten to the north wind sigh, And the wild geese call - ing.
'Neath the pear and ap - ple tree, See the ripe fruit heap - ing.

8

We plough the fields and scatter
The good seed on the land,
But it is fed and watered
By God's almighty hand:
He sends the snow in winter,
The warmth to swell the grain,
The breezes and the sunshine,
The soft refreshing rain:
All good gifts around us
Are sent from heaven above;
Then thank the Lord,
Oh, thank the Lord
For all his love.

                            —JANE M. CAMPBELL

Winter Comes

WORDS AND MUSIC
BY RAYMOND J. MALONE

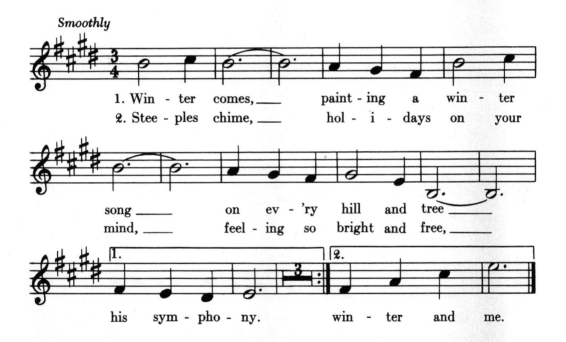

Smoothly

1. Win - ter comes, ___ paint - ing a win - ter
2. Stee - ples chime, ___ hol - i - days on your

song ___ on ev - 'ry hill and tree ___
mind, ___ feel - ing so bright and free, ___

[1.] his sym - pho - ny. [2.] win - ter and me.

This gentle song describes the beauty and joy of a winter season. The poem speaks of the snow of winter preparing the land for spring planting. What other moods do you associate with winter? Compare the songs on pages 27 and 157 with "Winter Comes."

Night Herding Song

COWBOY SONG

Slowly

1. Go slow, lit - tle do - gies, stop mill - ing a - round,
2. Lay down, lit - tle do - gies, stop shift - ing a - round,

I'm tired of your rov - ing all o - ver the ground.
Just stretch a - way out on the wide o - pen ground.

There's grass where you're stand - in', so feed kind - a slow,
My horse is leg - wea - ry and I'm aw - ful tired,

You don't have for - ev - er to be on the go,
If you get a - way I am sure to be fired,

Move slow lit - tle do - gies, move slow.__ Hi - o, hi - o, __ hi - o.__
Lay down, lit - tle do - gies, lay down.__ Hi - o, hi - o, __ hi - o!__

Many songs begin or end on **do.**
This song begins on **mi.**
What scale step is used
for the last note?

Evening Song

WORDS BY FANNIE STEARNS DAVIS
MUSIC BY RUTH DE CESARE

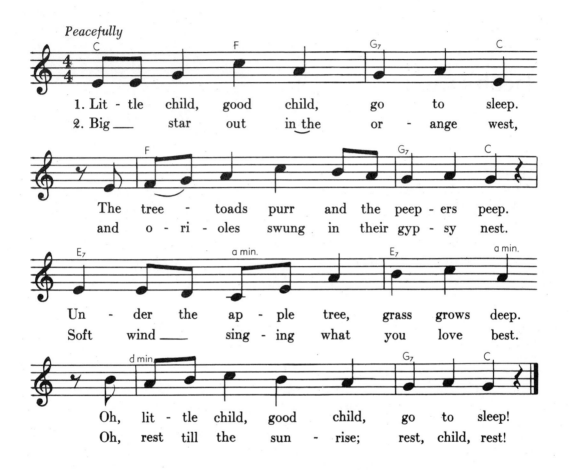

Peacefully

1. Lit - tle child, good child, go to sleep.
2. Big ___ star out in the or - ange west,

The tree - toads purr and the peep - ers peep.
and o - ri - oles swung in their gyp - sy nest.

Un - der the ap - ple tree, grass grows deep.
Soft wind ___ sing - ing what you love best.

Oh, lit - tle child, good child, go to sleep!
Oh, rest till the sun - rise; rest, child, rest!

3. Swift dreams swarm in a silver flight,
   Now, hand in hand with the sleepy night,
   Lie down soft with your eyelids tight.
   Oh, hush, child, little child!
   Hush! Good night.

Melodic phrases are not always repeated in a song.
Can you find any repeated phrases in "Evening Song"?

Jacob's Ladder

SPIRITUAL

Steadily

1. We are climb - ing Ja - cob's lad - der, We are
2. Ev - 'ry round goes high - er, high - er, Ev - 'ry
3. Sin - ner do you love your Je - sus? Sin - ner

climb - ing Ja - cob's lad - der, We are climb - ing
round goes high - er, high - er, Ev - 'ry round goes
do you love your Je - sus? Sin - ner do you

Ja - cob's lad - der,
high - er, high - er, } Sol - dier of the cross.
love your Je - sus?

4. If you love Him, why not save them?

5. We are climbing higher, higher.

We're on the Upward Trail

TRADITIONAL

We're on the up - ward trail! We're on the up - ward trail!

Sing - ing, sing - ing, Ev - 'ry - bod - y sing - ing, As we go!

We're on the up - ward trail! We're on the up - ward trail!

Sing - ing, sing - ing, Ev - 'ry - bod - y sing - ing, Home-ward bound!

Play the patterns below as you sing.
They will help to keep the rhythm steady,
particularly in the measures with whole notes.

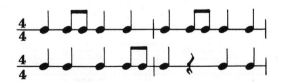

How would you describe the mood of this song?
Is the music better for square dancing or marching? Why?

From HAPPY DAYS, © 1942 Cooperative
Recreation Service, Inc., Delaware, Ohio.

The Alabama

SEA CHANTEY

This sea chantey reflects a gay, happy mood.
The melody should be sung very forcefully
while the smooth descant provides contrast.

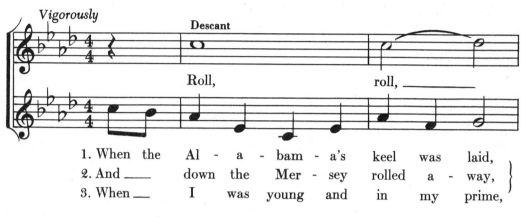

Vigorously

Descant

Roll,   roll, _____

1. When the Al - a - bam - a's keel was laid,
2. And ___ down the Mer - sey rolled a - way,
3. When ___ I was young and in my prime,

roll, _____   roll,   roll,

Roll, Al - a - bam - a, roll,

They ___ laid her keel in
And ___ sailed a - cross the
I ___ joined her on the

roll, roll, ___ roll, _____ roll!

Birk - en - head,
west - ern sea, Oh roll, Al - a - bam - a roll!
Black Ball Line,

14

Lament for a Donkey

WORDS ADAPTED BY MARTHA HARRIS
SPANISH FOLK TUNE

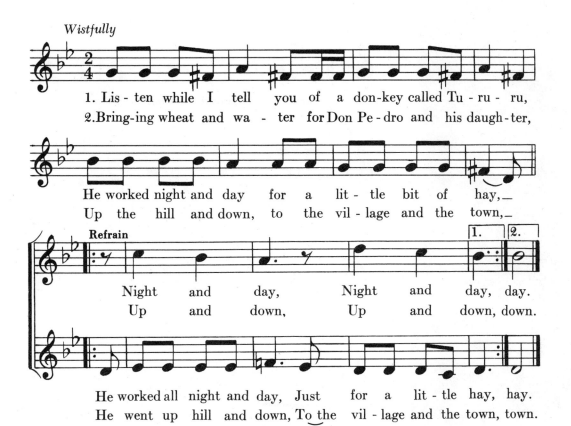

Wistfully

1. Lis - ten while I tell you of a don-key called Tu - ru - ru,
2. Bring-ing wheat and wa - ter for Don Pe - dro and his daugh-ter,

He worked night and day for a lit - tle bit of hay,—
Up the hill and down, to the vil - lage and the town,—

Refrain

Night and day, Night and day, day.
Up and down, Up and down, down.

He worked all night and day, Just for a lit - tle hay, hay.
He went up hill and down, To the vil - lage and the town, town.

3. One hot summer day, tho',
    Poor Tururu passed away, oh,
    He breathed weary sighs
    And forever closed his eyes.
    He breathed such weary sighs
    And forever closed his eyes.

    Descant: Closed his eyes.

4. All the village people
    Came together round the steeple,
    Said, "We'll ring the bell,
    For the donkey worked so well."
    They said, "We'll ring the bell,
    For the donkey worked so well."

    Descant: Ding, dong, bell.

Song of the River

WORDS BY FRANCIS ANDERSON
UKRANIAN FOLK MELODY

Slowly

1. Hark to the sound of rush - ing wa - ters,
2. No-where a man will brave the tor - rent,

Hear the great riv - er's might - y roar;
None but the wind can match its flight;

Black as the night it rac - es on - ward,
On - ly the moon's pale rays to watch them

On to the sea's far - dis - tant shore.
Speed through the dark and storm - y night.

Clair de Lune

BY CLAUDE DEBUSSY

"Clair de Lune" means moonlight. Debussy wrote several other pieces inspired by the moon. Some other composers who have written music which describes the moon in sound are Robert Schumann, Franz Schubert, and Anton Dvorák.

Debussy, who was one of the greatest French composers, wrote many pieces that are musical pictures of familiar things in the world around us. These pieces have titles such as "Gardens in the Rain," "Spring," "Flowers," "Gold Fish," "Footsteps in the Snow," and "Summer Nights." In these compositions, you can hear Debussy's impressions of the things mentioned in the titles.

Here is the first melody.

It begins with a wide ascending skip. The rest of the melody moves mainly by step in a descending line. Here you see contrast of direction and type of melodic movement. Contrast is one of the most important elements in music.

Here is the second melody.

You can see that it uses notes of longer time value. It also uses different rhythmic patterns. These are two more ways in which a composer provides contrast.

You can hear contrast as you listen to the music. The melody which opens the composition is first played by strings. When this melody returns toward the close of the recording, it is played by an oboe and flute. What other instrument do you hear several times?

How would you describe this music? Does it shimmer like moonlight? If you were a composer, what kind of sounds would you use to describe the moon?

Goodnight

WORDS BY ANGELA WOODS
GERMAN FOLK TUNE

Sing as smoothly and quietly as possible
to emphasize the dreamy mood of this song.

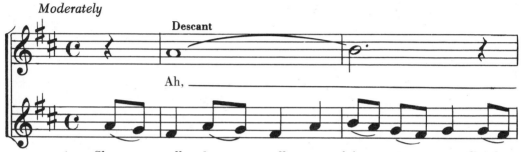

Ah, _____

1. Sleep __ well, sleep __ well, my fair - est __ one, Good -
2. Through the night all the earth is peace - ful and still, With __

_____ Ah, _____

night, my loved one true. Sleep __ well, sleep __ well, my
moon and stars a - bove. Dear- est one, may your sleep be

fair - est one, My __ dreams are all of you; May __
filled with dreams That __ tell you of my love; The __

18

an - gels guard your slum - ber deep, And__ o - ver you a
si - lent stars and moon so bright Will__ soon give way to

vig - il keep, Sleep__ well, sleep__ well,
morn - ing's light; As I wake with the dawn,

my fair - est__ one, Good - night, my loved one true.
my thoughts__ are of you, On - ly you, my loved one true.

The descant is a four note **ostinato.** To learn more about an **ostinato,** and how to write one, turn to page 140. Can you make up another **ostinato** using the same rhythm but different scale tones? Use F♯, G, and A. Which tone will you repeat every four measures?

This Land is Your Land

WORDS AND MUSIC
BY WOODY GUTHRIE

Steadily

1. This land is your land, __ This land is my land, __
2. As I went walk-ing __ that ribbon of high-way, __
3. When the sun came shin-ing __ And I was stroll-ing, __

From Cal - i - for - nia __ To the New York is - land, __
I saw a - bove me __ that __ end - less sky-way, __
And the wheat fields wav - ing __ And the dust clouds roll - ing, __

From the red - wood for - ests __ To the Gulf-stream wa - ters, __
I __ saw be - low me __ that gold - en val - ley, __
As the fog was lift - ing __ A __ voice was chant-ing, __

This land was made for you and me. __

20

MELODY IN MUSIC

Sidewalks of New York

WORDS BY CHARLES B. LAWLOR
MUSIC BY JAMES W. BLAKE

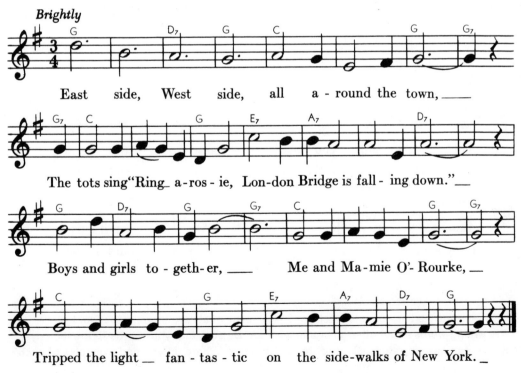

Brightly

East side, West side, all a - round the town, ____

The tots sing "Ring_ a-ros - ie, Lon-don Bridge is fall - ing down." __

Boys and girls to - geth- er, ____ Me and Ma - mie O'- Rourke, __

Tripped the light __ fan - tas - tic on the side-walks of New York. _

You Can Have One Wish

WORDS AND MUSIC
BY JOAN GARDNER AND
ADELAIDE HALPERN

Smoothly

1. If you had one wish, what would it be? Would you like
2. If you had one wish, what would it be? Would you like

a cas - tle by the sea? Or a gold - en throne
an ice - cream fac - to - ry? Or a big bal - loon

where you'd sit and rule a - lone? Would you like a stur - dy
you could fly in, to the moon? Would you like a box of

sail - ing ship you could cap - tain out to sea?
su - gar plums with a dia - mond lock and key?

If you real - ly had a spe - cial wish, what would it be?

What does the time signature tell you? How many beats are there in each measure?
Try writing words about other things to wish for. Be sure that your words fit the melody.
Melodies can move by steps, skips, or repeated tones. Where do you find examples of each?

22

To May

This flowing melody was written by Mozart,
a famous eighteenth-century composer.

WORDS BY GILBERT COOK
MUSIC BY W. A. MOZART

Happily

The win - ter days pass slow - ly, The ground lies fro - zen and white; ___ But then the earth a - wak - ens And flow - ers glad - den the sight. ___ For May comes soft - ly steal - ing And li - lac blos - soms ap - pear, ___ While vi - o - lets nod gen - tly To show ─ that spring-time is here.

You will see curved lines connecting some of the notes.
If the line connects two notes of the same pitch, it is a **tie**.
If the line connects two notes of different pitch, it is a **slur**.

A tie increases the length of the first note by that of the second.
A slur indicates that two or more tones are to be sung smoothly on one syllable.

Must I Then?

WORDS ADAPTED BY CLAUDIA REGEN
GERMAN FOLK SONG

Moderately

Must I then, must I then, say good-bye once a-gain,

good-bye a-gain, As I leave my home and you?

Tell me when, tell me when, if I come back a-gain,

come back a-gain, Will I find a heart that's true?

Not an-oth-er maid will I pur-sue

if I know that you care,— too.

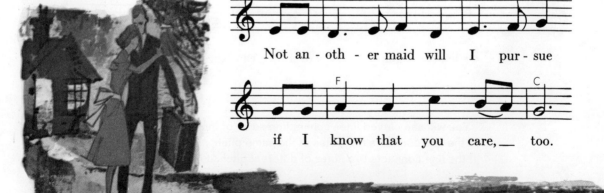

24

I'll know then, I'll know then, we will meet once a-gain,

meet once a-gain, And our love will be-gin a-new.

Taps

This song uses only **four** notes. It begins on **so.**

U.S. ARMY BUGLE CALL

Slowly

Day is done, Gone the sun, From the

lakes, from the hills, from the sky. All is

well, safe-ly rest, God is nigh.

My Homeland

WORDS BY FRANZ WILHELM
ARR. BY JOHANNES BRAHMS

Notice the irregular number of beats in the phrases of this melody. What is the time value of each of the rests?

Wistfully

1. In my home-land I long to be, Friends there a - wait me.
2. Though in dis - tance I'm far a - way, I'll re - turn some day.

Oh, my home-land, my home-land, My home-land so fair.

The Morn Doth Break

ENGLISH ROUND

Joyfully

The morn doth break and, far a - bove,

A sky - lark sings his song of love.

26

Lovely Maiden

WORDS BY HARRY G. TREBILCOX
MUSIC BY JOSEPH HAYDN

Here is a song with four unlike melodic phrases. The rhythmic patterns of these phrases are exactly alike.

Gaily

1. BOYS: Love - ly maid - en, let me in, For the night is freez - ing,
2. BOYS: Love - ly maid - en, don't be cruel, For with love I'm burn - ing,

Hear the howl - ing of the wind, Lis - ten to my sneez - ing.
O - pen wide your cot - tage door, Come and still my yearn - ing.

GIRLS: No, you can - not en - ter now, I can't help your numb - ness.
GIRLS: If with love you're burn - ing up, Then you can't be chill - y.

It's no fault of mine you're cold, It's your sim - ple dumb - ness.
Take your - self off to your bed, And don't act so sil - ly.

3. BOYS:
Lovely maiden, please be kind
To a humble baker.
I can give you only love,
I'm no money-maker.
GIRLS:
Bakers do not interest me,
You are but a dough man.
If you stand much longer there,
You will be a snow man.

4. BOYS:
Heartless maiden, hear me well,
I'll no more entreat you,
But I hope your husband's rich
And that he will beat you.
GIRLS:
Little baker, do not fret,
Rich or poor, no matter,
I am going to my bed,
You go to your batter.

The Piper's Song

WORDS AND MUSIC
BY ALFRED STERN

The **natural** sign in this song is an accidental. How does it affect the note? Be sure to hold the tied notes for their full value.

Briskly

Hear the pip-er's song, If you come, it won't be long,

Chil - dren, ___ come fol - low me. _____

You'll see a won-drous sight, You can stay a-wake at night,

Chil - dren, ___ come fol - low me. _____

You won't ___ be lone - ly, All girls and boys, ___

The place where we are go - ing ___ has all sorts ___ of toys. ___

Hear the pip - er's song, If you come, it won't be long,

Chil - dren, ___ come fol - low me. _____

Song of Fellowship

WORDS BY GEORGE K. EVANS
MUSIC BY W. A. MOZART

How would you compare this song
with Mozart's "To May" on page 23?

Slowly

Broth - er, take my __ hand in tok - en, May our

friend - ship __ ne'er be brok - en, Through the years to

come, __ we'll stay True and loy - al day by __ day, __

And our friend - ship's har - mo - ny __ will re - sound

e - ter - nal - ly, Will re - sound e - ter - nal - ly.

There are seven phrases in this melody.
The first two phrases have the same rhythmic pattern.
Can you find the one phrase which does not use eighth notes?
Can you find examples of other phrases which use different notes,
but have the same rhythmic patterns? Can you find the phrase that is repeated?
The use of repeated phrases and contrasting phrases adds interest and variety to music.

Lullaby of the Wind

The gently rocking quality of
the melody enhances the mood
of this soothing lullaby.

WORDS BY MADELEINE A. DUFAY
MUSIC BY MARY BECK STEVENS

Tenderly

1. Hush - a - by, hush - a - by, Soft winds sigh,
whis - p'ring by, Twi - light shad - ows bring an - gels near,
Stars are can - dles to guide them here. Soft winds sigh,
hush - a - by, Hush - a, hush - a - by. _____

2. Hushaby, hushaby,
   Soft winds sigh, whisp'ring by,
   Moonbeams open the gates of night,
   Clouds are curtains to hide their light,
   Soft winds sigh, hushaby,
   Husha, hushaby.

This music swings in twos. Sway back and forth, twice in each measure.
As you sway, tap this pattern quietly:

By doing this, you can feel the large and small divisions of each measure.

Sleep, My Little Bird

WORDS ADAPTED
BY HOLSAERT-BAILEY
YIDDISH FOLK SONG

A minor scale is used in this song
to fit the mood of the words.

Can you make up words to fit the melody
and the mood wherever "Eye lu lu lu lu" is sung?

From the collection, SING A SONG WITH CHARITY BAILEY,
© Plymouth Music Co.

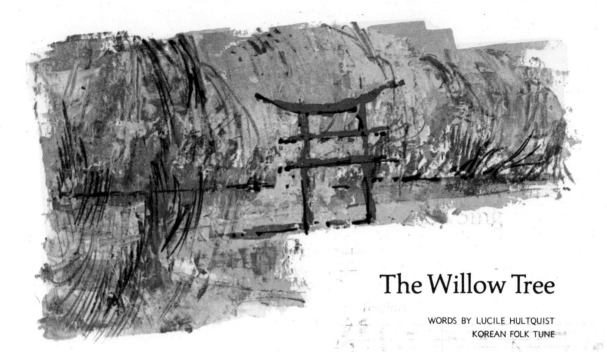

The Willow Tree

WORDS BY LUCILE HULTQUIST
KOREAN FOLK TUNE

Peacefully

In a gar-den, peace-ful and cool, Stands a wil-low tree,—

All its branch-es sweep to the ground, Hid-ing you and me;—

Qui-et-ness sur-rounds us here, In a leaf-y shade,—

In this en-chant-ed place, Mag-i-cal dreams are made.—

33

There's a Little Village

WORDS BY FLORENCE MARTIN
HAWAIIAN MELODY

Each phrase of this melody
begins with the three tones
that outline the I chord in G.

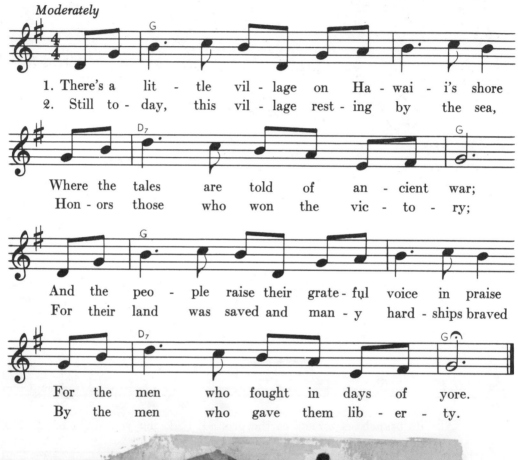

Moderately

1. There's a lit - tle vil - lage on Ha - wai - i's shore
2. Still to - day, this vil - lage rest - ing by the sea,

Where the tales are told of an - cient war;
Hon - ors those who won the vic - to - ry;

And the peo - ple raise their grate - ful voice in praise
For their land was saved and man - y hard - ships braved

For the men who fought in days of yore.
By the men who gave them lib - er - ty.

Song of Praise

This minor melody is gay and vigorous.
Hallelujah means "praise ye, the Lord."

PALESTINIAN FOLK SONG

Hal - le - lu - jah, hal - le - lu - jah, hal - le - lu jah, hal - le - lu!

Hal - le - lu - jah, hal - le - lu - jah, hal - le - lu - jah, hal - le - lu!

Hal - le - lu - jah, hal - le - lu - hal - le - lu - jah, hal - le - lu!

Hal - le - lu - jah, hal - le - lu - jah, hal - le - lu - jah, hal - le - lu!

The following patterns may be played as an accompaniment.
What other patterns can you make up, using only eighth and quarter notes?

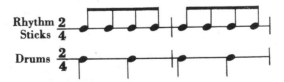

An accent mark (>) indicates that a note is to receive a slight stress.
There are many kinds of melodies. Melodies are often appealing because they are familiar, have interesting skips, or unusual rhythms. This melody is interesting because it uses only two different rhythmic patterns, many repeated notes, and a steady flow of eighth notes.

Reprinted rom GATEWAY TO JEWISH SONGS, by Judith Eisenstein, published by Behrman House, Inc. Used by permission.

To a Bird

WORDS BY MADELEINE A. DUFAY
MUSIC BY FREDERIC MISTRAL

Liltingly

1. Gay lit - tle bird, I know you're go - ing
2. Sweet lit - tle child, the sun I'll fol - low

O - ver a wide and dis - tant sea,
In - to a clear and bound - less sky,

Where you will find the warm winds blow - ing,
And with the lark, the wren, and swal - low,

Far from the sleep - ing flow - ers and me.
You'll hear our sum - mer song of good-bye;

Will you re - turn when leaves ap - pear __ and A - pril is here?
But we'll re - turn, **as** blos - soms do, __ to sing __ to you.

My Sailing Ship

WORDS BY T. V. VELOTTA
MUSIC BY GIOVANNI PAISIELLO

Gaily

1. My ship's so fair and free
2. My ship won't mind at all
3. And though my ship may be

And sails far out to sea,
If waves should rise or fall,
Not more than two feet three,

When o - cean breez - es are blow - ing,
Where an - gry wa - ters are flow - ing,
A cap - tain's pride I am show - ing,

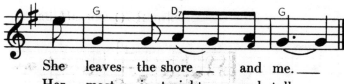

She leaves the shore ___ and me. ___
Her mast is straight ___ and tall. ___
As she sails back ___ to me. ___

37

Palomita Blanca

WORDS BY FRANCIS ANDERSON
SPANISH FOLK MELODY

One rhythmic pattern occurs three times in the melody. Clap or tap this pattern throughout the song.

1. Pa - lo - mi - ta blan - ca, Fly - ing through the sky,
2. Where can you be go - ing? Where will you a - light?
3. Pa - lo - mi - ta blan - ca, Al - ways fly - ing free,

Hear the song I sing to you As you wing by.
Will a new land greet you When you end your flight?
Will you cross the moun - tains Or come back to me?

Londonderry Air

IRISH FOLK SONG
ARRANGED BY GRAINGER

"Londonderry Air" is an old Irish folk tune from County Derry. You may know it as the song, "Danny Boy." This arrangement was made by Percy Grainger, who was a famous Australian pianist. The melody was a favorite of Grainger's and he also arranged it for piano, women's chorus, and mixed voices.

A melody must have certain features to be beautiful and lasting. Some of the features are movement and rest, change of direction, repetition, and variety. You can see that these features are like those of a good story or poem. As you listen to the recording, follow the shape of the melody with your hands.

RHYTHM AND DANCE

A Gypsy Tale

WORDS BY ANGELA WOODS
HUNGARIAN MELODY

Brightly

1. Once a smil - ing gyp - sy said to me,
2. "If you leave your trou - bles far be - hind,

"Come with us and share a life that's free;
Then a whole new world of joy you'll find;

Dance and sing, Laugh and be gay, Let bright

mu - sic drive your cares a - way." way." Hey!

Minka

WORDS BY JOHN HALL
RUSSIAN FOLK TUNE

When a melodic pattern is repeated, starting on a different note, it is called a **sequence**. There are several two-measure sequences in this gay minor song. How many can you find?

Allegro

1. Min - ka, Min - ka, when I leave thee, How my sad heart
2. When I hear sweet mu - sic play - ing, Ev - 'ry note to

al - ways grieves me, When I'm gone I long to be with
me is say - ing, "Min - ka, Min - ka, fair - est maid - en,

Min - ka, Min - ka mine. When I see the full moon shin - ing,
Min - ka, Min - ka mine." When the win - ter snow is fall - ing,

Then I will for thee be pin - ing, Min - ka, Min - ka,
I must go, for love is call - ing, Call - ing me to

fair - est maid - en, Min - ka, Min - ka mine.
be with Min - ka, Fair - est Min - ka mine.

There are different forms of minor scales. Look at the a minor scale on page 106. What tone is changed in the a minor scale used in "Minka"? How is the tone changed?

40

Four in a Boat

AMERICAN SINGING GAME

Brightly

1. Four in a boat and the tide rolls high, Four in a boat and the tide rolls high, Four in a boat and the tide rolls high, Wait - ing for a pret - ty girl to come by and by.

2. Choose your partner, stay all day,
   We don't care what the old folks say.

3. Eight in a boat and it won't go round,
   Swing that pretty one you've just found.

DANCE DIRECTIONS

Verse 1. Form a large circle with hands joined. Four players stand inside the circle.

The inside players bob up and down as the players in the circle run to the left.

Verse 2. The inside players choose partners who join them.
The players in the circle drop hands, reverse direction, and tiptoe to the right.

Verse 3. The inside players stand in place and sway from side to side until the last line.
Then they swing their partners. The players in the circle join hands again and
take two steps in and two steps out until the end of the verse. Repeat the game
with the first four inside players joining the circle.

41

Click, Go the Shears!

AUSTRALIAN BUSH BALLAD

Rhythmically

1. Down by the pen, there, the old shear - er stands,
2. Out on the floor in his cane - bot- tomed chair,
3. There is the tar - boy a - wait - ing com - mand,

Grasp - ing the shears in his thin bon - y hands.
There sits the boss with his eyes ev - 'ry - where.
With his black tar - pot and black tar - ry hands.

Fixed is his gaze on the next sheep to come;
Notes well each fleece as it comes to the screen
See! One old sheep with a cut on its back:

In a lit - tle min - ute, boys, an - oth - er's done.
Pay - ing strict at - ten - tion that it's tak - en clean.
Here is what he's wait - ing for, It's "Tar here, Jack!"

Refrain

Click   go   the   shears,   boys,   click,   click,   click!

Wide   is   his   blow   and   his   hands   move   so   quick.

The   ring - er   looks   a - round   and   is beat - en   by   a   blow.

Zip!   An - oth – er   sheep   is   done,   and   watch   him   go!

Short rhythmic patterns are often repeated in a song.
One pattern found in many songs is the dotted eighth and sixteenth:
How often does the pattern occur in this song? Can you find it in a descending scale?

I's the B'y

NEWFOUNDLAND BOAT SONG

"Sods and rinds" are the dirt and bark
used to cover the "flake," a platform
or rack on which fish are dried.

1. I's the b'y that builds the boat, And I's the b'y that
2. Sods and rinds to cover your flake, And cake and tea for
3. I took Li - zer to a dance, And, faith, but she could

sails her, I's the b'y that catch - es the fish And
sup - per, Cod - fish in the spring of the year, ____
trav - el, Ev - 'ry step that she ____ did take Was

takes 'em home to Li - zer.
fried in New - fie but - ter. } Hip yer part - ner, Sal - ly Tib - bo,
up to her knees in grav - el.

Hip yer part - ner, Sal - ly Brown! Fo - go, Twil - lin - gate,

More - ton's Har - bour, All a - round the cir - cle!

Fogo, Twillingate, and Moreton's Harbour
are all fishing towns in Newfoundland.

Oh, Paloma

TRANS. BY ETHEL CROWNINSHIELD
SOUTH AMERICAN FOLK MELODY

The first two measures of each phrase
have the same rhythmic pattern. Sing
the small notes softly, like an echo.

re - mem-ber you,
will come to you,

Smoothly

1. Oh, Pa - lo - ma, I re - mem - ber you, _____
2. Oh, Pa - lo - ma, I will come to you, _____

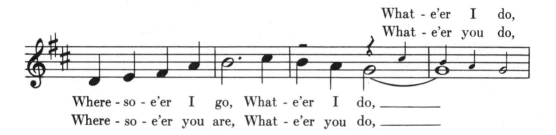

What - e'er I do,
What - e'er you do,

Where - so - e'er I go, What - e'er I do, _____
Where - so - e'er you are, What - e'er you do, _____

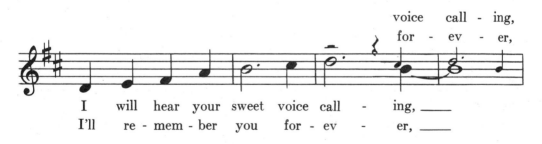

voice call - ing,
for - ev - er,

I will hear your sweet voice call - ing, _____
I'll re - mem - ber you for - ev - er, _____

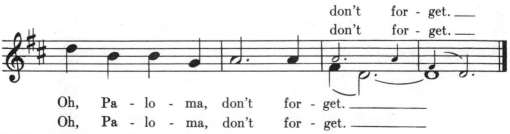

don't for - get. _____
don't for - get. _____

Oh, Pa - lo - ma, don't for - get. _____
Oh, Pa - lo - ma, don't for - get. _____

Off to the Army

WORDS BY ELOISE WILLIAMS
MUSIC BY W. A. MOZART

In Mozart's comic opera, "The Marriage of Figaro," Figaro sings this song to a young boy who is leaving to join the army.

Soon the long care - free days will be end - ing,

To the work of a sol - dier at - tend - ing;

March e - rect with a gun on your shoul - der,

And it's off to the ar - my you'll go;

March e - rect with a gun on your shoul - der,

And it's off to the ar - my you'll go.

What rhythmic pattern is used throughout the song?

Marching to Pretoria

How are the rhythmic and melodic
patterns of the verse and
refrain different?

WORDS AND MUSIC
BY JOSEF MARAIS

Lively

1. I'm with you and you're with me and so, we are all to-geth-er,
2. I love food and you love food and so, we shall eat to-geth-er,

So, we are all to-geth-er, So, we are all to-geth-er,
So, we shall eat to-geth-er, So, we shall eat to-geth-er.

Sing with me, I'll sing with you and so, we will sing to-geth-er,

Refrain

As we march a-long. ___ We are march-ing to Pre-to-ri-a, ___

Pre-to-ri-a, ___ Pre-to-ri-a, ___ We are march-ing

to Pre-to-ri-a, ___ Pre-to-ri-a, Hur-rah! ___

Pawpaw Patch

TRADITIONAL

Brightly

G   C   G   D₇

1. Where, oh where is sweet lit-tle Nel-lie? Where, oh
2. Come on, boys,— let's go— find her, Come on,
3. Pickin' up paw-paws, putt'n'em in her pock-et, Pickin' up

1. Where, oh where? Where,
2. Come on, boys, Come
3. Paw - paw patch, Paw -

a min.   D₇   G   C

where is sweet lit - tle Nel - lie? Where, oh where is
boys,— let's go— find her, Come on, boys,—
paw-paws, putt'n'em in her pock - et, Pickin' up paw-paws,

oh where? Where, oh
on, boys, Come on,
paw patch, Paw - paw

sweet lit-tle Nel-lie?
let's go___ find her,
putt'n'em in her pock-et,
} Way down yon-der in the paw-paw patch.

where?
boys,
patch,
}

Way down yon-der in the paw-paw patch.

DANCE DIRECTIONS

Form two lines with the boys on the right side of the girls.

Measures:

1—2   The first girl turns to her left and skips to the end of the line.

3—4   The first boy turns to his right and skips to the end of the line.

5—6   The first boy and girl join hands and take four sliding steps back to their original place at the beginning of the line.

7—8   The same couple takes four sliding steps back to the end of the line.

Repeat the steps until all the couples have had a chance to lead.

49

Coffee Grows on White Oak Trees

AMERICAN FOLK SONG

Smoothly

Refrain

Cof - fee grows on white oak trees, The riv - er flows with hon - ey - o, Go choose some - one to roam with you as sweet as 'las - ses can - dy - o!

Verse
Same tempo, but detached

1. Two in the mid - dle and they can't get o - ver, Two in the mid - dle and they can't get o - ver, Two in the mid - dle and they can't get o - ver, Oh, my Lil - ly, oh!

2. Swing you an - oth - er one and you'll get o - ver, Swing you an - oth - er one, and you'll get o - ver, Swing you an - oth - er one and you'll get o - ver, Oh, my Lil - ly, oh!

3. Four in the middle and they all get over,
   Four in the middle and they all get over,
   Four in the middle and they all get over,
   Oh, my Lilly, oh!

4. Four do-si-do and jump for joy,
   Four do-si-do and jump for joy,
   Four do-si-do and jump for joy,
   Oh, my Lilly, oh!

Chebogah

There are two different accidentals
in this song. Each appears in front
of a C. How do they affect the note?

WORDS ADAPTED
BY JOHN HALL
HUNGARIAN FOLK DANCE

Left __ slide, __ sev - en times, __ Don't be slow;

Right __ slide, __ sev - en times, __ Back we go;

Ver - y slow, ver - y slow, To the cen - ter glide;

Back a - gain, back a - gain, Part - ners side by side.

La Cucaracha

WORDS BY FLORENCE MARTIN
MEXICAN FOLK TUNE

Lively

1. Oh, the ti - ny *cu - ca - ra - cha* Is a fun - ny
2. Oh, the bus - y *cu - ca - ra - cha* Is a rov - ing

lit - tle bug, Peek - ing from be - hind the wood - work, Scoot - ing
vag - a - bond! Go - ing where he is - n't want - ed, Grab - bing

un - der - neath the rug. He's a dash - ing lit - tle trav - 'ler!
food of which he's fond. He must al - ways keep a - mov - ing,

Loves to live just like a king, In the ver - y fin - est
He can nev - er stop to rest; If he did, some - one would

plac - es, He de - vours ___ ev - 'ry - thing! ___
catch him, He is noth - ing but a pest! ___

Many Latin American songs use dance rhythms.
Can you make up a dance for "La Cucaracha"?

Refrain

La cu - ca - ra - cha, la cu - ca - ra - cha,

Scur - ries up and scur - ries down! La cu - ca - ra - cha,

la cu - ca - ra - cha, Home is an - y part of town!

La cu - ca - ra - cha, la cu - ca - ra - cha,

Has his trou - bles and his woes! La cu - ca - ra - cha,

la cu - ca - ra - cha, Hunt - ed ev - 'ry - where he goes!

This Train

SPIRITUAL

This pattern ♩ ♩ ♩ stresses the second beat, a weak part of the measure. This type of rhythmic pattern is known as **syncopation.**

Rhythmically

GIRLS: 1. This train is bound for glo - ry,
BOYS: 2. This train won't pull no ex - tras, } this train, ___

This train is bound for glo - ry,
This train won't pull no ex - tras, } this train, ___

This train is bound for glo - ry, If you ride it, you
This train won't pull no ex - tras, Don't pull noth - in' but the

must be ho - ly, This train is bound for glo - ry,
mid-night spe - cial, This train won't pull no ex-tras, } this train.___

3. GIRLS: This train don't pull no sleepers, this train,
   This train don't pull no sleepers,
   Don't pull nothin' but the righteous people,

4. BOYS: This train don't pull no jokers, this train,
   This train don't pull no jokers,
   Neither don't pull no cigar smokers,

54

This train!

ALL: 5. This train is bound for glo - ry, this train! _____

This train!

This train is bound for glo - ry, this train! _____

This train is bound for glo - ry, if you ride it you

must be ho - ly, This train is bound for glo - ry,

This train!

(Shout)

this train! _____ This train!

How many different train sounds
can you imitate on your rhythm instruments?

You can play this pattern on sand blocks to imitate the sound of a train.

Some of the class might speak the words "chug, chug, chug, chug," throughout the song.
Use the same pattern of eighth notes. This could also be used as an introduction or coda.

55

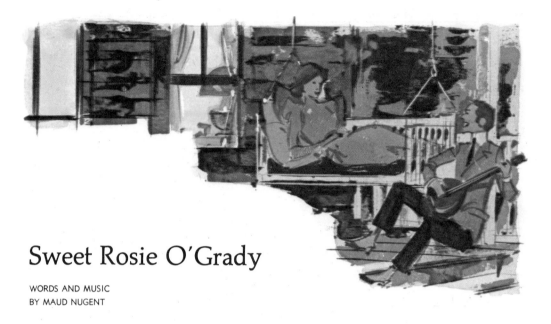

Sweet Rosie O'Grady

WORDS AND MUSIC
BY MAUD NUGENT

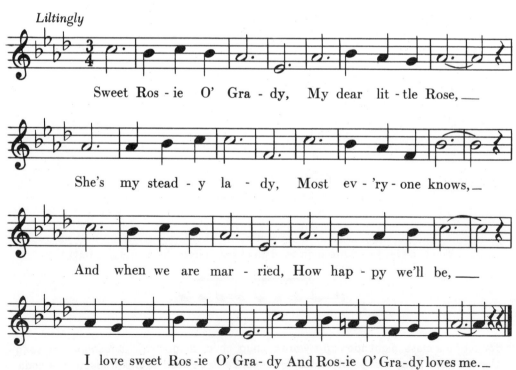

Liltingly

Sweet Ros-ie O' Gra-dy, My dear lit-tle Rose, ___

She's my stead-y la-dy, Most ev-'ry-one knows, ___

And when we are mar-ried, How hap-py we'll be, ___

I love sweet Ros-ie O' Gra-dy And Ros-ie O' Gra-dy loves me. ___

Fiesta Drum Song

Rebozas are gaily colored scarves.
A **fiesta** is a holiday or festival.

WORDS BY LUCILE HULTQUIST
PANAMANIAN FOLK TUNE

Steadily

1. R-r-rum-pa-dum! This is fi - es - ta, And the
2. R-r-rum-pa-dum! The girls all gath- er In their
3. See the dan- cers whirl -ing gai - ly While gui-

lit - tle drums are drum-ming. Come quick-ly and join us
col - or - ful *re - bo - zas.* The chil- dren are beat- ing
tars are sweet - ly strum-ming. There's sing- ing and laugh-ter

in the fun. For the car - ni - val is com - ing.
on their drums And the la - dies all toss ros - es.
all day long And the lit - tle drums are drum-ming.

Three of the four phrases in this song have the following rhythmic pattern:

Which phrase has a different pattern? Try using this pattern for a coda or introduction.

The Sailor

WORDS BY JOY RUNION
MUSIC BY MILDRED M. VANDENBURGH

Can you find any rhythmic patterns in
"The Sailor" that are also used
in the song on page 44?

Lively

To sail the sea is the life for me! The wind's

en - chant - ing song __ of pi - rates bold, __ of chests of gold,

Of strands of pearls this long, __ Make me wish I could be

a fish And search the depths be - low, __ To see if tales

that are told by gales Are real - ly, tru - ly so. __

Out in the Forest

The refrain of this song contrasts
sharply with the music of the verses.
Make up a dance to fit this gay song.

POLISH FOLK SONG

1. Out in the for - est, Mu - sic is ring - ing,
2. What ho, my gyp - sies! Where are you go - ing?

Gyp - sies are gath - 'ring, Laugh - ing and sing - ing.
Through-out the wide world, Glad - ness be - stow - ing.

Refrain

Boom - di - ar - i - ar - i, Boom - di - ar - i - ar - i,

Boom - di - ar - i - ar - i, Boom, Zip, Zip,

Boom - di - ar - i - ar - i, Boom - di - ar - i - ar - i,

Boom - di - ar - i - ar - i, Boom, Zip. Boom, Zip.

Across the Plain

WORDS BY HARRY G. TREBILCOX
CZECHOSLOVAKIAN FOLK TUNE

To imitate the sound of galloping
horses, tap this pattern as you sing.

Lively

1. Come, join with us and ride a - long. Sing a song of
2. Bright stars will guide us through the night. Sing a song of

friend - ship! Sing a song of broth- er-hood! Come, join with us
friend - ship! Sing a song of broth- er-hood! Bright stars will guide

and ride a - long, Let the whole world ech- o to our song.
us through the night, As we ride be-neath their sil- ver light.

Refrain

Hold - ing your hor - se's mane, Dash - ing a- cross the plain,

Sing - ing a wild re - frain, Swift as the wind we ride, —

Rid - ing the live - long day, Throw- ing our cares a - way,

60

Sing - ing   this   roun - de - lay,   Ride   side   by   side.

Awake!

WORDS BY G. A. STUDDERT-KENNEDY
GERMAN MELODY

This song has an unusual time signature.
How many beats will there be in each measure?
What kind of note will get one beat?
Does the music swing in twos or threes?

1. A - wake, a - wake __ to love   and work, The   lark   is
2. To   give   and give, __ and give   a - gain, What God   hath

in __ the   sky, __   The   fields   are   wet __ with dia - mond dew,
giv - en   thee; __   To   spend   thy - self __ nor count the cost,

The   worlds   a - wake __ to   cry _____   Their   bless - ings
To   serve   right   glo - rious - ly _____   The   God __ who

on __ the   Lord   of   Life, __   As   He   goes meek - ly   by. __
gave __ all   worlds   that   are, __   And   all   that   are   to   be. __

© Hodder and Stoughton Ltd., London, England,
and Harper and Brothers, New York, N. Y.

61

Danca Brasileira

BY CAMARGO GUARNIERI

This "Brazilian Dance" was composed by Guarnieri, a contemporary composer who was born in Brazil in 1907. He has written orchestral music, piano pieces, songs, and concertos. This piece is a samba, a popular dance which originated in Brazil.

Three characteristics of the samba are a fast tempo, rhythmic patterns which use notes of equal time value, and *syncopation*. Syncopation is a rhythmic pattern in which the accents fall on a weak beat or weak part of a beat instead of on the strong beat or strong part of the beat.

There are two melodies in this composition.
One consists of notes of even time value moving at a fast tempo.

This first melody is accompanied by rhythm instruments playing the syncopated patterns necessary to the samba. Here are the two patterns we hear:

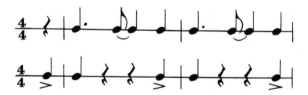

The second melody is syncopated.

At the end of the composition both themes are played together.

Latin American music uses percussion instruments to increase the rhythmic interest. How many different percussion instruments can you identify as you listen?

Oh, Come Play a Merry Tune

WORDS ADAPTED BY RENE MARTIN
FRENCH FOLK TUNE

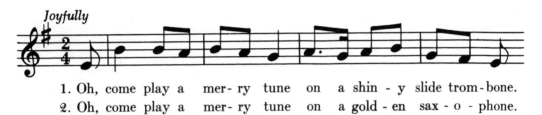

1. Oh, come play a mer-ry tune on a shin-y slide trom-bone.
2. Oh, come play a mer-ry tune on a gold-en sax-o-phone.

Oh, come play a mer-ry tune on a shin-y slide trom-bone.
Oh, come play a mer-ry tune on a gold-en sax-o-phone.

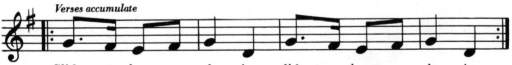

Slide trom-bones are play-ing, slide trom-bones are play-ing,
Sax-o-phones are play-ing, sax-o-phones are play-ing,

Oh, oh, oh! Make the mer-ry mu-sic flow.

3. . . . on a lively clarinet.
   Clarinets are playing,

4. . . . on a booming kettledrum.
   Kettledrums are playing,

Musical Instruments

Cello

The cello is too large to be held under the chin like a violin. A spike supports the cello at the bottom, while the body of the cello is held between the knees of the performer. Cello tone can be either dark and mellow or quite brilliant in quality, depending upon the register.

RANGE

To avoid reading too many leger lines, three different clefs are used: bass, treble, and tenor. In the tenor clef, middle C is found on the fourth line.

Tenor Clef

Flute

The flute is one of the oldest wind instruments. The earliest flutes were made from wood or cane, but today they are usually made of silver.

The flute is often used to play solo passages. Its lower tones are subdued, its middle tones are sweet and mellow, and the upper tones are very brilliant.

RANGE

The tone is produced by blowing air across an opening near one end of the instrument. To sound different pitches, the player presses keys which close or open holes found at various places along the flute. Most orchestras use two or three flutes.

Trombone

The trombone is different from other brass instruments because the player changes the pitch by using a slide to lengthen or shorten the tubing. This slide is made of two brass tubes, one fitting inside the other. There are no valves or keys on the trombone.

Sound is produced by the vibration of the player's lips inside a mouthpiece shaped like a small cup.

RANGE

The trombone can produce tones that are capable of overpowering an entire orchestra. Its soft tones sound like a soft organ tone. An orchestra will usually use three trombones.

Snare Drum

The snare drum looks much like a small bass drum. However, it is mounted on a stand, with the playing head at the top. Sound is produced by striking the drum head with two wooden sticks.

The lower head has strings of metal sretched across its underside. These strings are called snares. When the player strikes the playing head with the sticks, the air inside the drum vibrates. The vibrating air causes the lower head to push against the snares. This makes the dry rattling sound characteristic of the snare drum. If the snares are loosened when the drum is struck, a softer tom-tom sound is produced.

Oom-Pa-Pa

WORDS AND MUSIC
BY ALFRED STERN

Briskly

You play oom - pa - pa, I'll play oom - pa - pa,

You play oom - pa - pa and we'll all dance.

When I play oom - pa - pa, ___ all the girls sing, "La, la,

la," ___ and dance to oom - pa - pa, ___ it's such a thrill. ___

The girls do toe and heel ___ while the boys get down and kneel, _

how hap - py oom - pa - pa ___ will make you feel. ___

A - round and round you twirl, __ hang - ing on to ev - 'ry girl, __

Nev - er had such mer - ry fun, __ oom - pa - pa ev - 'ry - one.

Now throw your hats up high, __ till they al - most hit the sky __

and dance to oom - pa - pa, ___ oom - pa - pa - pa. __

2. You play oom-pa-pa, I'll play oom-pa-pa,
   You play oom-pa-pa, and we'll all dance.
   When I play oom-pa-pa, All the boys shout rah, rah, rah,
   For when you oom-pa-pa, it's so much fun.
   The boys get down and kneel
   While the girls do toe and heel,
   How happy oom-pa-pa will make you feel.
   Now take your partner's hand,
   Turn around, it's simply grand,
   For the fun has just begun,
   Oom-pa-pa ev'ry one.
   Now throw your hands up high,
   Till they almost reach the sky,
   And dance to oom-pa-pa, oom-pa-pa-pa.

Oom-pa-pa sounds like a tuba.
Ta-ta-ta-ta-ta sounds like a trumpet.
Can you make sounds like a bass drum or a flute?

Dance of the Toy Flutes

FROM "THE NUTCRACKER SUITE"
BY PETER TCHAIKOVSKY

Peter Ilyitch Tchaikovsky was a well-known Russian composer of the nineteenth century. He wrote all types of music. Among his most famous compositions are his ballet scores. A ballet tells a story through dancing. Ballet does not use sung or spoken lines. The story must be told through the dancer's movements.

The "Nutcracker Ballet" is the story of Marie, a little girl who dreams that all her Christmas toys and gifts have come to life and dance for her. The Russian doll dances a *trepak*, the flowers perform a waltz and, in this piece, three flutes perform a light, delicate dance.

There are two melodies in this piece. The first one is played by three flutes. Because they are playing in a high register, the flutes have a brilliant sound.

Here is the second melody. How does it contrast with the first melody? Can you name the instrument which plays this melody?

After the second melody, you will hear the first melody again. If the first melody is called A, and the second melody B, you will see that the composition is in A—B—A form. Composers repeat melodies to give unity to their music. They use new melodies to add contrast. The way melodies are repeated or contrasted is what determines the form of a composition.

All types of art have *form* which is created from two basic elements—variety and unity. In music we hear, rather than see, form. Colors are created by sounds, rather than brushes. Now look at the picture on pages 20 and 21. Here is a piece of art you can see. How many elements of variety and unity can you find? Examine the picture for color, lines, curves, and balance.

In Bahia Town

WORDS BY ROBERTA McLAUGHLIN
BRAZILIAN FOLK TUNE

Refrain

La la la la la, La la la la la, La la la la la la.

Melody Instrument

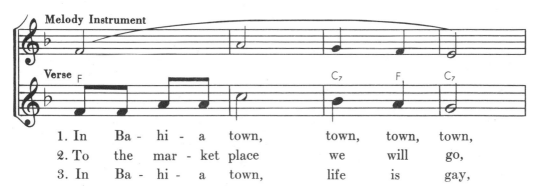

Verse

1. In Ba - hi - a town,   town,   town,   town,
2. To the mar - ket place   we   will   go,
3. In Ba - hi - a town,   life   is   gay,

Buy ba - nan - as ev - 'ry day, co - co - nuts so brown.
In the pla - za we will find fresh - est fruit, I know.
You'll be danc - ing in the street, *fies - tas* ev - 'ry day.

Used by Permission of Bowmar Records.

Number Twenty-Nine

WORDS AND MUSIC
BY W. S. HAYS

Make up an accompaniment for
the refrain using bells and
whistles as suggested by the
words. Accompany the verses
with sticks or sand blocks.

Allegro

C melody instrument

1. Roar-ing through the for-ests, Glid-ing through the vale,
2. She's a thing of beau-ty, Fly-ing o'er the road,
3. Hark! I hear her com-ing, Through the si-lent night,

Slip-ping through the tun-nels, Fly-ing o'er the rail;
Belch-ing forth her pow-er, With her heav-y load;
Don't you hear her whis-tle? Don't you see the light?

Train be-hind her danc-ing All a-long the line;
Eas-y in her mo-tion, Per-fect in de-sign,
Here she comes, she's fly-ing, With the train be-hind.

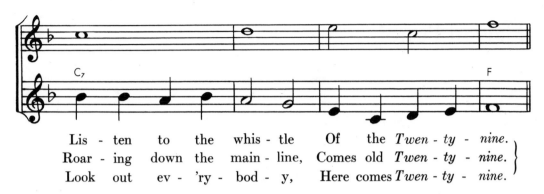

Lis - ten to the whis - tle Of the *Twen - ty - nine.*
Roar - ing down the main - line, Comes old *Twen - ty - nine.*
Look out ev - 'ry - bod - y, Here comes *Twen - ty - nine.* }

Refrain

Clear the track! Here she comes!

Clear the track the bell is ring - ing! Here she comes on time!

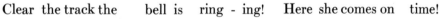

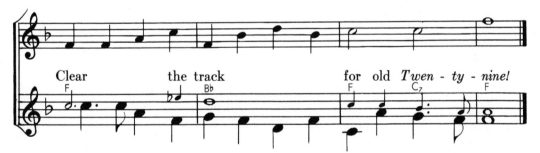

Clear the track the whis - tle's blow - ing for old *Twen - ty - nine!*

This song reviews many things you have studied. What does the time signature tell you?
How does the flat sign affect the note in the fourth measure from the end of the song?

In what key is this song written? What is the home tone? Clap the rhythms of the
refrain. Half of the class may clap the descant while the rest clap the melody.
How does a dot affect the value of a note? Give the dots full time value.

Hawaii Ponoi

WORDS BY HELENA HARGRAVE
HAWAIIAN MELODY

Ha - wai - i, land we love, Fair as the heav'ns a-bove,

What friend - ly shores are thine, A - lo - ha land!

We will be ev - er true To our red, white, and blue,

And serve with faith - ful hearts. Ha - wai - i Nei.

The ukulele is a good instrument to use for accompanying Hawaiian songs.

Ancient Wisdom

WORDS BY ROBERTA McLAUGHLIN
CHINESE MELODY

Softly

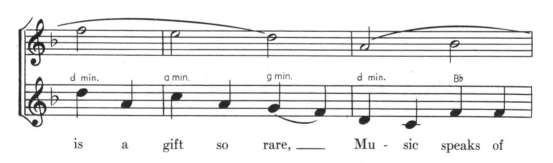

Mu - sic is a bond that binds us, Mu - sic

is a gift so rare, ___ Mu - sic speaks of

har - mo - ny ___ Link - ing earth and man to heav - en. ___

Used by Permission of Bowmar Records.

A Life on the Ocean Wave

WORDS AND MUSIC
BY HENRY RUSSELL

1. A life on the o - cean wave, __ A __ home on the roll - ing deep, __ Where __ scat - tered wa - ters rave, __ And __ winds their rev - els keep. __ Like an ea - gle caged, I

2. Once more on the deck I stand, __ Of __ my own swift glid - ing craft, __ Set sail! Fare - well to the land, __ The gale fol - lows far __ a - baft. __ We shoot thru the spark - ling

3. The land is no more in view, __ The __ clouds have be - gun to frown; __ But with a stout ship and crew, __ We'll say, "Let the storm __ come down!" __ And the song of our heart shall

pine __ On this dull, un-chang-ing shore, __ Oh, give me the
foam, __ Like an o - cean bird set free, __ And, like the sea
be, __ While the winds and wa - ters rave, __ A life on the

flash - ing brine, __ The spray and the tem - pest roar. __
birds, our home __ We'll find far out on the sea. __
heav - ing sea, __ A home on the bound - ing wave. __

A life on the o - cean wave, __ A __ home on the roll - ing deep, __

Where the scat - tered wa - ters rave __ And __ winds their rev - els keep. __

Fifty Stars

WORDS AND MUSIC
BY E. J. HERMANN

Steadily

Fif - ty stars, ___ thir-teen bars, ___ It's a grand flag that

waves o'er the land of the brave. Col - ors three, _____

Fine

fly - ing free, _____ Sym-bol of our lib - er - ty.

1. From Maine's rock - y land to Ha - wai - i's sun - ny sand,
2. The first min - ute man fought to lib - er - ate his land,

From the south - ern key to po - lar sea,
And a peo - ple free we'll al - ways be.

Stars and Stripes Forever

BY JOHN PHILIP SOUSA

The names of Johann Strauss and Stephen Foster usually bring to mind waltzes and ballads. The name John Philip Sousa makes us think of marches and band music. Sousa's fame rests almost entirely on his marches, while his songs, operettas, and orchestral music are practically forgotten.

Sousa was born in Washington, D. C. in 1854. He was bandmaster of the United States Marine Corps Band from 1880 to 1892. In 1892 he formed his own band which was very popular and successful both in this country and in Europe.

Here are two of the main melodies used in "Stars and Stripes Forever."
Look at them before listening to the music. How do they differ?
Are the ranges different? Do they use accidentals or different rhythmic patterns?

A march will usually have a time signature of $\frac{4}{4}$, $\frac{2}{4}$, $\frac{6}{8}$ or ¢.

All of these time signatures indicate that there are either two or four beats in each measure. If you try to march to music with a time signature showing three beats in a measure, your marching will feel very stiff and unnatural. Alternating a strong beat with a weak beat is one of the characteristics of the march.

The Village Square

WORDS BY EDWINA WELLS
MUSIC BY J. P. RAMEAU

Rameau was a famous French composer
of the eighteenth century. He wrote
operas, ballets, and harpsichord music.

Gaily

1. When the tam - bou - rines and pipes start play - ing,
2. Hear the hap - py shouts and laugh - ter ring - ing,

And the joy - ful mu - sic fills the air,
No one has a wor - ry or a care.

Mer - ry danc - ers come with - out de - lay - ing,
Join - ing in the danc - ing and the sing - ing,

For a cel - e - bra - tion in the vil - lage square.
At the cel - e - bra - tion in the vil - lage square.

Make up a rhythmic accompaniment for the second
half of this song. What other instruments could
be used to accompany a Creole folk song?

Zuzette

WORDS BY YVONNE CARR
CREOLE FOLK TUNE

Rhythmically

1. Oh, Zu - zette, why are you so mourn - ful?
2. Oh, Zu - zette, won't you be more cheer - ful?

Oh, Zu - zette, *chère a - mie,* Why are you so blue?
Oh, Zu - zette, *chère a - mie,* What more can I do?

Moun - tains I will climb, *chère a - mie,*
Moun - tains I did climb, *chère a - mie,*

Corn stalks I will bind, *chère a - mie,*
Corn stalks I did bind, *chère a - mie,*

Mon - ey I will find, *chère a - mie,* All to give to you.
Mon - ey I did find, *chère a - mie,* All of this for you.

79

Leader Man

WORDS AND MUSIC
BY ROSE MARIE COOPER

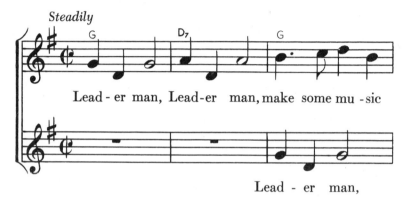

Lead - er man, Lead - er man, make some mu - sic

Lead - er man,

if you can. I'll sing high, you sing low,

Lead - er man, make some mu - sic if you can,

and we'll all end up to - geth - er.

and we'll all end up to - geth - er.

HARMONY IN MUSIC

The More We Get Together

GERMAN FOLK SONG

Gaily

The more we get to - geth - er, to - geth - er, to - geth - er;

The more we get to - geth - er, the hap - pier are we!

For your friends are my friends, and my friends are your friends,

The more we get to - geth - er, the hap - pier are we!

The following descant may be sung or played on a melody instrument.
The descant pattern should be repeated four times during the song.

Sing to - geth - er

The Count of Cabra

WORDS BY FLORENCE MARTIN
SPANISH FOLK TUNE

Boys may sing "Oh, yes ma'am" and
girls may sing "Oh, yes sir" in
place of the words **de veras.**

Rhythmically

BOYS: I'm the Count of Ca - bra, *de ver - as!*
GIRLS: I would like to mar - ry, *de ver - as!*
MOTHER: Don't ig - nore this of - fer, *de ver - as!*

Will you mar - ry me? I'll be the best
Quick - ly as I can. It's not you I'll
This is what I say, You must be a

hus - band, *de ver - as!* This you well can see.
mar - ry, *de ver - as!* I've an - oth - er man.
count - ess, *de ver - as!* There's no oth - er way.

4. GIRLS: Riches, jewels, titles, *de veras!*
        Never won my heart,
        But I'll wed the Count *(sniff)*, *de veras!*
        Love plays not a part.

5. BOYS: So it's me you'll marry, *de veras!*
        Brave and handsome me!
        I'm the finest husband, *de veras!*
        You will ever see.

Chungala

Chungala means "Oh, pretty girl."
In what key is this song?
Name the home tone.

WORDS BY ANGELA WOODS
SPANISH FOLK MELODY

Happily

Hear the joy - ful cho - rus ring - ing, Come and

join the hap - py sing - ing, May our friend - ship last for -

ev - er, Let us play and sing to - geth - er,

Oh, chun - ga - la, oh, chun - ga - la, la;

Oh, chun - ga - la, oh, chun - ga - la; Oh, chun - ga - la,

oh, chun - ga - la, la; Let us play and sing to - geth - er.

Spanish melodies are often **harmonized in thirds.** This means the added part follows
the shape of the melody but is written and sung two scale steps above or below the melody.

Big Rock Candy Mountain

AMERICAN FOLK SONG

Rhythmically

1. On a sum - mer day in the month of May, A —
2. Oh, a farmer and his son, they were on the run To the

bur - ly bum came hik - ing Down a shad - y lane
hay - field they were bound- ing; Said the bum to the son,

thru the sug - ar cane; He was look - ing for his lik - ing;
"Why — don't you come To that big rock can - dy moun - tain?"

As he roamed a - long, he sang a song Of a
So the very next day they hiked a - way, The —

land of milk and hon - ey, Where a bum can stay for —
mile- posts they kept count - ing, But they never ar - rived at the

man - y a day, And he won't need an - y mon - ey.
lem - on - ade tide On the big rock can - dy moun - tain.

Refrain

Oh, the buz - zin' of the bees in the sug - ar plum trees,

Near the so - da wa - ter foun - tain, At the lem - on - ade

springs, where the blue - bird sings, On the big rock can - dy moun - tain.

Buy My Apples

WORDS BY YVONNE CARR
FRENCH FOLK TUNE

You might add rhythmic interest to
the middle section of this song
with an accompaniment using the
eighth- and sixteenth-note rhythm
found in the first measure.

Red ap - ples, green ap - ples, Yel - low ones, too,

Come buy my ap - ples, buy them do; Who will buy my ap - ples?

All kinds of ap - ples I'll sell to you.

Red ones and green ones, yel - low ones, too, They are good for you.

This one you bake, and that one you fry; but

this is the best one for ap - ple pie.

Alleluia

WORDS BY W. S. HAYNIE
MUSIC BY JOSEPH HAYDN

Reverently

1. Al - le - lu - ia, al - le - lu - ia,
2. Al - le - lu - ia, al - le - lu - ia,

Praise __ the Lord, __ the Lord __ on high, __
Now __ the time __ has come __ to sing, __

Al - le - lu - ia, Al - le - lu - ia,
Al - le - lu - ia, Al - le - lu - ia,

Lord __ of earth __ and Lord __ of the sky.
Lift __ your voice __ in praise __ of the King.

The Old Chisholm Trail

COWBOY SONG

Chisholm is pronounced chizzum.
A leader may sing the verses with
the group singing the chorus.

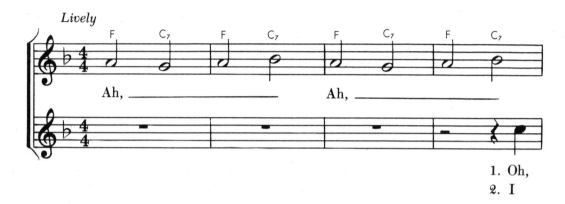

Ah, _____ Ah, _____

1. Oh,
2. I

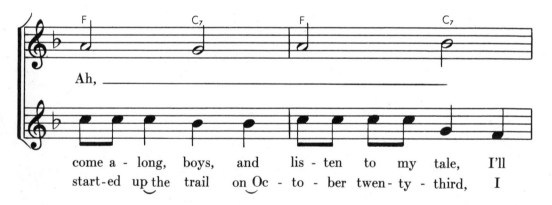

Ah, _____

come a - long, boys, and lis - ten to my tale, I'll
start-ed up the trail on Oc - to - ber twen - ty - third, I

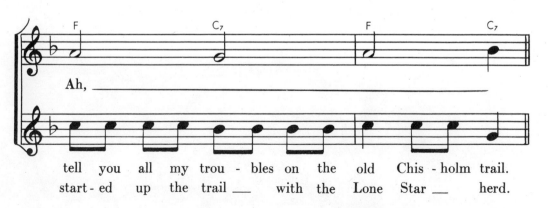

Ah, _____

tell you all my trou - bles on the old Chis - holm trail.
start-ed up the trail ___ with the Lone Star ___ herd.

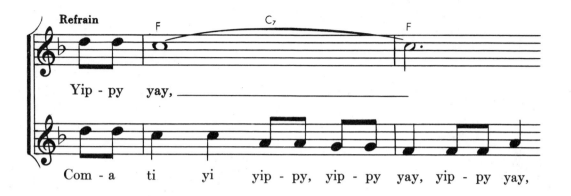

Yip - py yay, _____

Com - a ti yi yip - py, yip - py yay, yip - py yay,

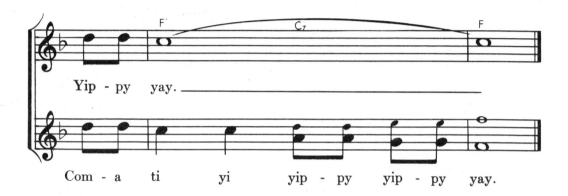

Yip - py yay. _____

Com - a ti yi yip - py yip - py yay.

3. I woke up one morning on the old Chisholm trail,
   With a rope in one hand and a cow by the tail.

4. I'm up in the mornin' before daylight,
   And before I sleep the moon shines bright.

5. It's bacon and beans most every day,
   I'd just as soon be eatin' prairie hay.

6. I' goin' back to town to draw my money,
   I'm goin' back home to see my honey.

7. I'll sell my outfit just as soon as I can,
   And I won't punch cattle for any man.

8. With my knees in the saddle and my home in the sky,
   I'll quit punching cows in the sweet bye and bye.

Ha! Ha! Ha!

WORDS ADAPTED BY JOHN HALL
SWEDISH FOLK TUNE

A dot placed over or under a note is called a **staccato mark.** It tells you to sing or play the note in a short, detached manner.

Rhythmically

C Melody   F   G₇

1. Ha ha ha! He he he! Sing - ing all to - geth - er, sing - ing
2. Ha ha ha! He he he! Lis - ten to the laugh - ter as you

Ha ha ha! He he he! Ha   ha   ha!

C   C   F   G₇   C

mer - ri - ly!   Ha ha ha! He he he! Ho ho ho! Mer - ri - ly.
sing with me.

He he he!   Ha ha ha! He he he! Ho ho ho! Mer - ri - ly.

A few students might sing or play this four-note ostinato throughout the song.
Sing the **ostinato** as smoothly as possible.

Sing mer - ri - ly!

While the Miller Sleeps

WORDS BY MARGARET LOWREY
FRENCH FOLK TUNE

Notice the change of meter, the fermata signs, and the D.C. al Fine in this song.

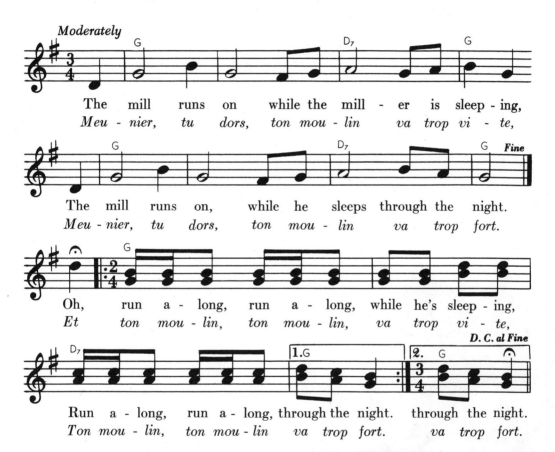

Moderately

The mill runs on while the mill - er is sleep - ing,
Meu - nier, tu dors, ton mou - lin va trop vi - te,

The mill runs on, while he sleeps through the night.
Meu - nier, tu dors, ton mou - lin va trop fort.

Oh, run a - long, run a - long, while he's sleep - ing,
Et ton mou - lin, ton mou - lin, va trop vi - te,

D. C. al Fine

1. Run a - long, run a - long, through the night. 2. through the night.
Ton mou - lin, ton mou - lin va trop fort. va trop fort.

Come A-Riding

WORDS BY ALICE SNYDER KNUTH
CZECHOSLOVAKIAN FOLK TUNE

Make up an instrumental accompaniment
using sticks, sand blocks, and bells
to imitate the sound of horses' hooves.

Gaily

1. Come a- rid - ing   in the morn-ing, Far from my fa-ther's house,
2. We come rid - ing   in the morn-ing, Back to my fa-ther's house,

Jin - gle, jan - gle,   on our hors - es,   Ring bells so gay.
Jin - gle, jan - gle,   on our hors - es,   Ring bells so gay.

Rid - ing,   Rid - ing,

Pranc - ing light - ly   on the wide high road,
Rid - ing, rid - ing   on the long home road,

Rid - ing,   Rid - ing,

Turn down   on a   green by - road,
Leav - ing   the ___ lone by - road,

Rid - ing,   Rid - ing,

Rid - ing o - ver   hills we   love to roam, Care - free our · way.
Smell the cook - ing   as we   near our home, Oh, hap - py day!

Zum Gali Gali

ISRAELI FOLK SONG

The rhythmic **ostinato** accompanying this melody may also be used as an introduction and coda.

Moderately

Melody

1. He - cha lutz le 'man a - vo - dah; _____
2. A - vo - dah le 'man he - cha - lutz; _____

Zum ga - li, ga - li, ga - li, Zum ga - li, ga - li,

_____ A - vo - dah le 'man he - cha - lutz.
_____ He - cha - lutz le 'man a - vo - dah.

Zum ga - li, ga - li, ga - li, Zum ga - li, ga - li.

Only after verse 4

Zum ga - li, ga - li, ga - li, Zum ga - li, ga - li, Zum. ___

3. He - cha - lutz le 'man ha - b'tulah;
Ha-b'tulah le 'man he-cha-lutz.

4. Ha-sha-lom le 'man ha'a-mim;
Ha'a-mim le 'man ha-sha-lom.

93

School Days

WORDS BY WILL D. COBB
MUSIC BY GUS EDWARDS

The harmony part in this song
moves mostly by half steps.
Where does it move by whole steps?

Liltingly

School   days, school days, dear old gold - en rule   days,

Read - in' and 'rit - in' and 'rith - me - tic, Taught to the

tune of a hick - 'ry stick, You were my queen in cal - i - co,

I was your bash - ful bare - foot beau, And you wrote on my

slate, "I love you, Joe," When we were a   cou - ple of kids. _____

The first two measures of this
song may be sung or played as
an introduction, a coda, or as
an **ostinato** figure throughout.

Are You Sleeping?

FRENCH FOLK TUNE

Brightly

Ding, ding, dong; Ding, ding, dong, Are you sleep - ing, Are you sleep - ing,

Broth - er John, Broth - er John? Morn - ing bells are ring - ing,

Morn - ing bells are ring - ing, Ding, ding, dong; Ding, ding, dong.

This song is fun to sing as a four-part round in different languages.
Everybody may sing the introduction, or you may begin at Roman numeral I.

FRENCH
Fre - re Jac-ques, Fre - re Jac-ques,
Dor-mez vous? Dor-mez vous?
Son-nez les ma-tin-nes, (twice)
Ding, din, don! Ding, din, don!

GERMAN
Bru-der Jak-ob, Bru-der Jak-ob,
Schlaefst du noch? Schlaefst du noch?
Mor-gen glock-en leu-ten, (twice)
Bim, bam, boom! Bim, bam, boom!

SPANISH
Fray Fe-li-pe, Fray Fe-li-pe,
Duer-mus tu'? Duer-mus tu'?
To-ca la cam-pa-na, (twice)
Tan, tan tan! Tan, tan, tan!

The Dairy Maids

WORDS BY JAMES SLOCUM
ENGLISH FOLK TUNE

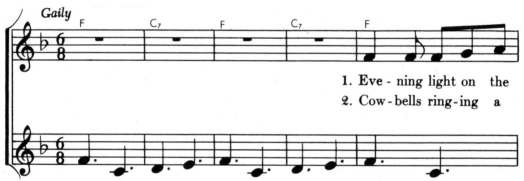

1. Eve - ning light on the
2. Cow - bells ring-ing a

1. Twin - kling, twin-kling, Twin-kling, twin-kling, Twin - kling,
2. Tin - kling, tin - kling, Tin - kling, tin - kling, Tin - kling,

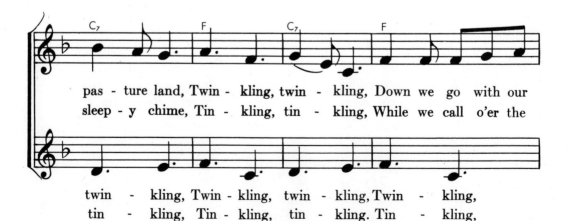

pas - ture land, Twin - kling, twin - kling, Down we go with our
sleep - y chime, Tin - kling, tin - kling, While we call o'er the

twin - kling, Twin - kling, twin - kling, Twin - kling,
tin - kling, Tin - kling, tin - kling. Tin - kling,

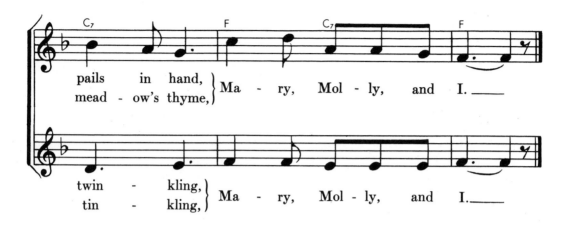

pails in hand,
mead - ow's thyme, } Ma - ry, Mol - ly, and I.____

twin - kling,
tin - kling, } Ma - ry, Mol - ly, and I.____

3. Making butter's the best of fun,
   Churning, churning,
   Oh, we're sorry when summer's done,
   Mary, Molly, and I

The last two measures of this round outline the tones of the I chord in the key of F major. On what scale step does the round begin?

Brothers

TRADITIONAL ROUND

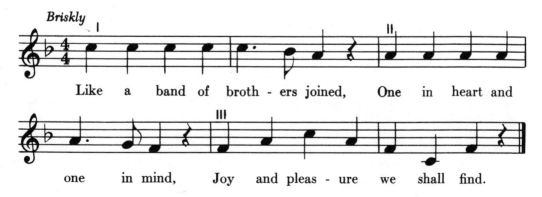

Like a band of broth - ers joined, One in heart and

one in mind, Joy and pleas - ure we shall find.

Finlandia

BY JAN SIBELIUS

In the late nineteenth century, many composers began to use native folk tunes to express national traits and legends in music. The movement started in Czechoslovakia, Russia, and Scandinavia and was called Nationalism. It spread rapidly to other parts of the world. Events from national history were used as subjects for operas and *program music*.

Program music is inspired by a particular story, mood, or idea. Composers who wish to honor their homeland have often done so by writing program music. One of the most popular pieces of program music is the *tone poem* "Finlandia" by Sibelius. Tone poems are orchestral pieces usually written in one movement. "Finlandia" was composed in 1890 during a period of national strife. It portrays three different moods: tragedy, courage, and hope. Listen to the three melodies and picture the three contrasting moods of the music.

Can you identify the instrument that plays each of these themes?
How does the tone color of these instruments affect the mood?

How does Sibelius use changes of tempo, rhythm, and dynamics to help convey the different moods?

The third theme has had words added to it and is often printed in hymnals.
It has become one of the most popular national songs of Finland.
Notice that the melodic movement of this tune is mainly by step.

READING MUSIC

Reading the following song will be easier if you find the three phrases that are alike. Which of the four phrases is different?

Joyful, Joyful, We Adore Thee

WORDS BY THE REV. HENRY VAN DYKE
MUSIC BY LUDWIG VAN BEETHOVEN

Moderato

Joy - ful, joy - ful, we a - dore Thee, God of Glo - ry, Lord of Love;

Hearts un - fold like flow'rs be - fore Thee, O - pen to the sun a - bove.

Melt the clouds of sin and _ sad - ness; Drive the _ dark of doubt a - way;

Giv - er of im - mor - tal glad - ness, Fill us with the light of day!

Does the melody move mostly by steps, by skips, or repeated tones?
What does the meter signature tell you?
Most of the notes are quarter notes and get one beat.

Every note in the following song is found in the I chord in the key of C.

do—mi—so—do
1 3 5 8
C E G C

Sing We Rejoicing

TRADITIONAL

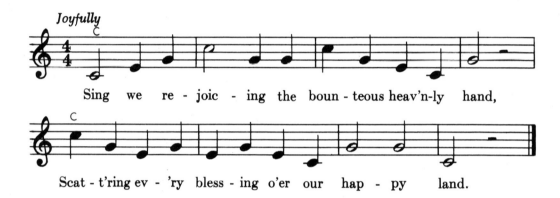

Sing we re - joic - ing the boun - teous heav'n-ly hand,

Scat - t'ring ev - 'ry bless - ing o'er our hap - py land.

What is the home tone? Sing the song with syllables or numbers.

Here is another song. This one is in the key of F. The home tone is F.

Frogs

OLD ROUND

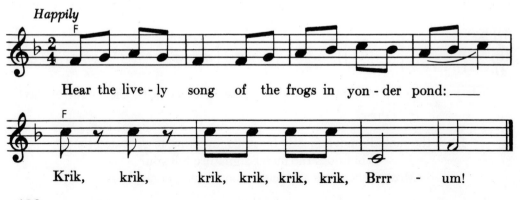

Hear the live - ly song of the frogs in yon - der pond: ____

Krik, krik, krik, krik, krik, krik, Brrr - um!

You can build a major scale on any tone, using the same order of whole and half steps used in building a scale on C. Make sure that there is a half step between 3—4 and 7—8.

Play a major scale starting on F. You must flat the B in order to make a half step between 3 and 4.

Using a flat (♭) *lowers the tone* a half step.

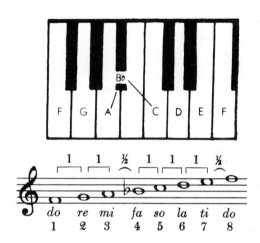

Since a B♭ is needed to play or sing in the key of F major, this flat is placed at the beginning of each staff, following the treble clef sign.

This is called the *key signature*. It means that every B is flatted.

Here is the key signature for the key of F:

I chord

Read this song in the key of F:

Whistle, Mary, Whistle

AMERICAN FOLK SONG

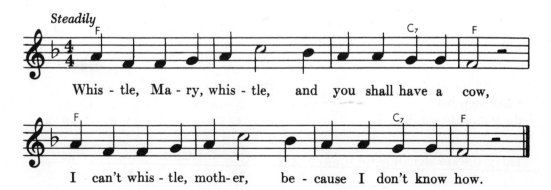

Whis - tle, Ma - ry, whis - tle, and you shall have a cow,

I can't whis - tle, moth-er, be - cause I don't know how.

Here is a song in the key of G. The home tone is G.

In Poland There's an Inn

WORDS ADAPTED
MUSIC BY JOHANNES BRAHMS

Moderato

In   Po - land there's an   inn, In   Po - land there's an   inn,

In   Po-land there's a Po - lish inn,Where Po- lish sol-diers stout and thin

Are   al - ways flock- ing   out   and in, for - ev - er   out and   in.

Play the G major scale on piano
or on bells.

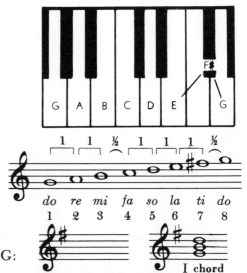

Some key signatures have sharps.
Using a sharp (♯) *raises the tone
a half step.*

You will see that in order to make
a half step between 7 and 8
the F must be raised to F♯.

This is the key signature for the key of G:

102

A song can be written in any key. When a song is written in a different key, the new key signature tells you the scale on which the song is built and where the home tone is.

Sing this phrase of the song you learned in the key of F. In what key is it now?

Hear the live - ly song of the frogs in yon - der pond: ____

When we change the key of a song, it is called *transposition*.
Songs are transposed to suit the different ranges of various kinds of voices or instruments. When you sing the phrase of "Frogs" transposed to G, you have to sing higher than when you sing the same phrase in the key of F.

This song in the key of G is a lullaby.

Sleep, Baby, Sleep

WORDS BY W. G. WHITTAKER
GERMAN FOLK SONG

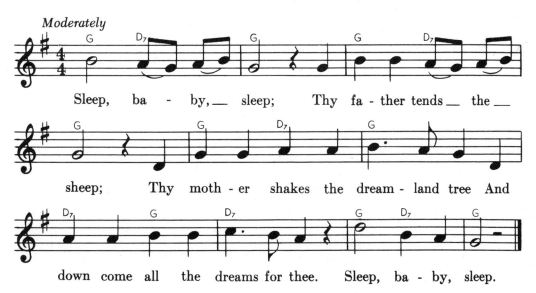

Sleep, ba - by, __ sleep; Thy fa - ther tends __ the __

sheep; Thy moth - er shakes the dream - land tree And

down come all the dreams for thee. Sleep, ba - by, sleep.

Many things you have learned about reading music are found in "America."

America

WORDS BY SAMUEL L. F. SMITH
MUSIC BY HENRY CAREY

In what key is this song written? What does the time signature tell you?
Remember, the upper number tells you how many beats there are in a measure.
The lower number tells you the kind of note that gets one beat.

The time signature of "America" is called "three four."

This is the dotted half note. A dot increases the length of the note by
one-half its value. In time signatures in which the quarter note gets
one beat, the dotted half note gets three beats.

You will see another rhythmic pattern in "America."

This is the dotted quarter and eighth note. (♩. ♪)

Two eighth notes (♪ ♪) are equal to a quarter note (♩). In $\frac{2}{4}$, $\frac{3}{4}$, and $\frac{4}{4}$ time, two eighth notes receive one beat.

♩ ♫   This pattern equals two beats.

♩ ♫   This pattern also equals two beats.

♩ ♪   This is the same pattern written an easier way.
        The dot has the same value as the eighth note.

♩.   This is a dotted quarter note. It receives one and one-half beats.

Clap or chant these rhythms:

Here are some melodies to read that use dotted quarter notes. Sing with syllables or numbers.

Most of the songs you have read use the tones of the major scale. Some songs you have sung use tones of the *minor scale*.

You can play a minor scale on the piano by starting on A
and playing all the white keys to the next A.

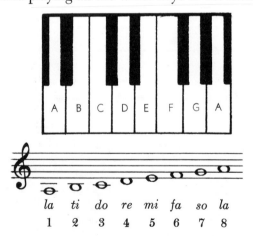

la	ti	do	re	mi	fa	so	la
1	2	3	4	5	6	7	8

Play this scale and listen to it.
It does not sound like a major scale.

Now sing this song in a minor key.

The Wind

WORDS AND MUSIC
BY HARRY R. WILSON

The cold wind is sing - ing a sol - i - tar - y mourn - ful song.

You may know the following song as sung in a major key.
Sing it in minor and hear how different it sounds.

Intry Mintry

TRADITIONAL

In - try min - try cu - try corn, Ap - ple seed and ap - ple thorn,

Wi - re bri - ar lim - ber lock, Five wild geese all in a flock.

Turn and turn and turn a - bout, o - u - t and it spells "out."

Here are some melodies for you to read. Before you sing each one, find the home tone and name the key. Not all start on the home tone. Some begin on *mi* or *so*.

110

FORM IN MUSIC

The Silver Birch

WORDS ADAPTED BY MARCELLA BANNON
RUSSIAN FOLK TUNE

Moderately

1. Sil - ver birch a - lone in a mead - ow,
2. Un - der - neath the tree he is rest - ing,
3. In the mead - ow mu - sic is ring - ing,

Stand - ing all a - lone in a mead - ow,
'Neath the shad - y tree he is rest - ing,
Sweet en - chant - ed mu - sic is ring - ing,

Soon a shep - herd boy comes stroll - ing,
Takes a branch a - bove him sway - ing,
From the leaves so soft - ly sigh - ing,

With his sheep and goats he's stroll - ing.
Carves a lit - tle pipe for play - ing.
To the shep - herd's pipe re - ply - ing.

Ol' Texas

COWBOY SONG

On a piece of paper, draw a dash to represent the time value of each note. You will notice similar patterns occurring every two measures.

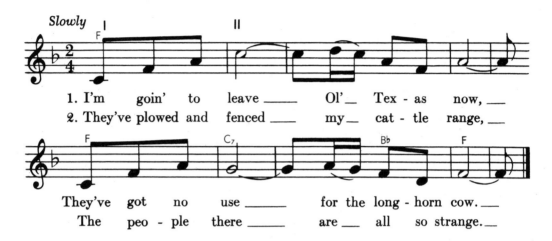

1. I'm goin' to leave ____ Ol' ___ Tex - as now, ____
2. They've plowed and fenced ____ my ___ cat - tle range, ____

They've got no use ____ for the long - horn cow. ____
The peo - ple there ____ are ___ all so strange. ____

The songs on these two pages are **rounds.** Rounds are written for two, three, or more groups of singers. Everyone sings the same melody but each group begins at a different time. You should always learn the entire melody before trying to sing a round in parts.

If the round, "Ol' Texas," were written out, it would look like this.

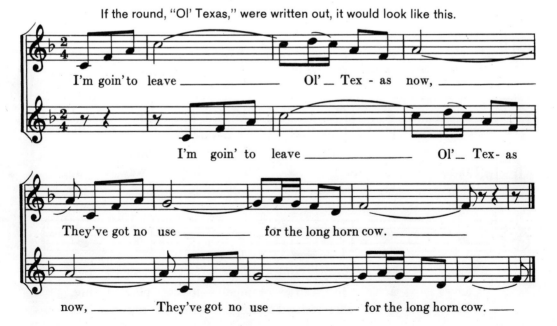

I'm goin' to leave _____ Ol' ___ Tex - as now, _____

I'm goin' to leave _____ Ol' ___ Tex - as

They've got no use _____ for the long horn cow. _____

now, _____ They've got no use _____ for the long horn cow. ____

Moonlight

There are two sequences of the first
two measures. Where do they occur?

ITALIAN ROUND

Gracefully

While all the world lies dream-ing, I sail the moon-lit wa-ters,

A path of sil-ver gleam-ing to guide me on-ward.

The Bell Doth Toll

This round is in three parts.
The third section has a
contrasting rhythmic pattern.

ENGLISH ROUND

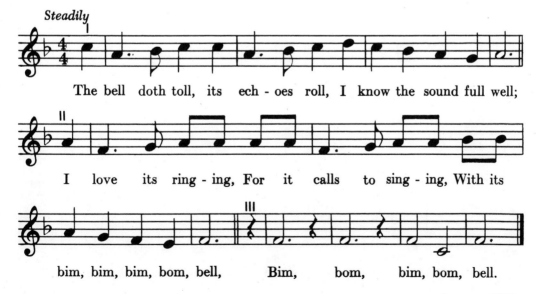

Steadily

The bell doth toll, its ech-oes roll, I know the sound full well;

I love its ring-ing, For it calls to sing-ing, With its

bim, bim, bim, bom, bell, Bim, bom, bim, bom, bell.

113

Roll On, Columbia

WORDS AND MUSIC
BY WOODY GUTHRIE

This song is in two sections. The general outline of the melodic and rhythmic patterns is very similar. What differences can you find?

1. Green Doug - las fir where the wa - ters cut through,
2. Oth - er big riv - ers add pow - er to you,

Down her wild moun - tains and can - yons she flew,
Yak - i - ma, Snake, and the Klick - i - tat, too,

Ca - na - di - an North - west to the o - cean so blue,
Sand - y, Wil - lam - ette, and the Hood Riv - er, too,

Refrain

Roll on, Co - lum - bia, roll on. ___ Roll on, ___ Co - lum - bia, roll on,

Roll on, ___ Co - lum - bia, roll on, Your pow - er is turn - ing our

dark - ness to dawn. Roll on, Co - lum - bia, roll on. ___

3. At Bonneville now there are ships in the locks,
   The water has risen and covered the rocks,
   Shiploads a-plenty are soon past the docks,
   Roll on, Columbia, roll on.
   (Refrain)

4. And on up the river is the Grand Coulee Dam,
   The biggest thing built by the hand of a man,
   To run the great fact'ries and to water the land,
   Roll on, Columbia, roll on.
   (Refrain)

Sailing

FROM "HARBOR VIGNETTES"
BY HERBERT DONALDSON

You should be familiar with the A—B—A form explained on page 68. In this piece by Herbert Donaldson, a contemporary American composer, you will learn about a new form, the *rondo*.

The rondo alternates one theme with two or more different themes. The rondo form in "Sailing" is A—B—A—C—A.

Here is the A theme. Listen for it to come back.

In the B theme you will hear violins. This section is called "Seagulls."
You will hear a piano in the C theme. This section is called "Flying Fish."

You might think of the form of the piece like this:
A   B   A   C   A
Sailing—Seagulls—Sailing—Flying Fish—Sailing

When you listen to music, try to hear the form by comparing the themes.
It will make your listening more interesting.

115

Shadow Song

WORDS AND MUSIC
BY JOAN GARDNER AND ADELAIDE HALPERN

Many popular songs are written in
A-B-A form. A repeat of the first
eight measures makes the first A
sixteen measures long. Both B and
the second A are eight measures long.

Liltingly

Let's walk a - long, two by two, sing - ing a song
They'll nev - er talk or com - plain, They like to walk

like the quar - tets do; You sing high, I'll sing low,
in the wind or rain, They will glide by our side,

and our shad - ows will fol - low a - long.
Yes, our shad - ows will fol - low a - long.

It might be kind of lone-some with just you and me, But

when we're all to - geth - er, We know that four is com- pan - y!

To - night the moon should be new, Let's make a wish

and they'll both wish, too. One's like me, one's like you,

And our shad - ows do ev - 'ry - thing we do. _____

Faith of Our Fathers

WORDS BY F. W. FABER
MUSIC BY H. F. HEMY AND J. G. WALTON

There are six phrases in this song. Two of them are exactly alike. Can you find three contrasting rhythmic patterns?

1. Faith of our fa - thers, liv - ing still
2. Faith of our fa - thers, we __ will love

In spite of dun - geon, fire __ and sword,
Both friend and foe in all __ our strife,

Oh, how our hearts __ beat high __ with joy
And preach thee, too, __ as love __ knows how,

When - e'er we hear that glo - rious word!
By kind - ly words and vir - tuous life.

Refrain

Faith of our fa - thers, ho - ly faith,

We will be true to thee till death.

Children of the Heavenly Father

TRANS. BY ERNST W. OLSON
SWEDISH FOLK SONG

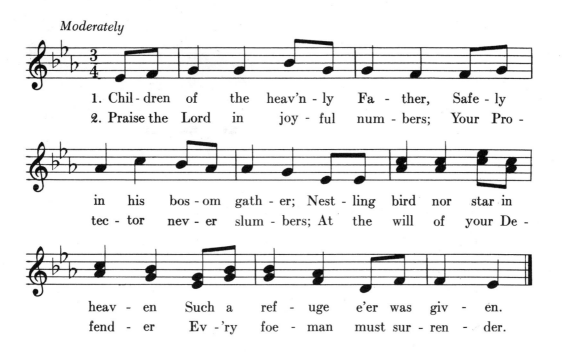

Moderately

1. Chil-dren of the heav'n-ly Fa - ther, Safe-ly
2. Praise the Lord in joy-ful num-bers; Your Pro -

in his bos-om gath - er; Nest-ling bird nor star in
tec - tor nev - er slum - bers; At the will of your De -

heav - en Such a ref - uge e'er was giv - en.
fend - er Ev -'ry foe - man must sur - ren - der.

3. God His own doth tend and nourish;
   In His holy courts they flourish.
   From all evil things He spares them,
   In His mighty arms He bears them.

4. Though He giveth or He taketh,
   God His children ne'er forsaketh,
   His the loving purpose solely
   To preserve them pure and holy.

Each of the four phrases in this song uses the same rhythmic pattern.

119

DRAMA AND MUSIC

Nocturne

FROM "MIDSUMMER NIGHT'S DREAM"
WORDS BY MADELEINE A. DUFAY
MUSIC BY FELIX MENDELSSOHN

Slowly

Twi- light comes and now the sun's gold - en light fades a - way,
Birds a - light on dark-'ning branch - es, all seek - ing their nests,

1.

The deep - en - ing shad - ows en - fold the dim - ming day,____
And down in the mead - ow, the

2.

drow - sy crick - et rests, Hear the wind, to nod - ding flow - ers

whis - per of day's sur - ren - der, See a ray of bril - liant

sun - shine en - throne a fad - ing cloud in splen-dor, in fleet - ing

splen - dor, Stars ap - pear and fill the heav - ens with bright sil - ver

glow, The moon keeps a vig - il o'er sleep - ing earth be - low.

Meet Me in St. Louis, Louis

FROM "MEET ME IN ST. LOUIS"
WORDS BY ANDREW B. STERLING
MUSIC BY KERRY MILLS

Cheerfully

Meet me in St. Lou - is, Lou-is, Meet me at the fair. __

Don't tell me the lights are shin-ing an - y place but there. __

We'll have so - da pop and can - dy, ___

And the night will be just dan - dy,

If you will meet me in St. Lou - is,

Lou - is, Meet me at the fair. __

A Village Holiday

A PLAYLET WITH SONGS FROM YOUR BOOK

CHARACTERS

BILL, a city boy   BERT, a country boy
JANE, his sister   SALLY, his sister
DOWDY DAN, a hobo   GRANDMA GRUNTS
SAM, a storekeeper   Three Dairy Maids

The curtain opens on an empty, old-fashioned village store. Behind a counter are shelves stocked with canned goods, etc. Bill and Jane enter.

(Song: "It's a Hap-Hap-Happy Day," p. 4.)

JANE: I wonder where everybody is?
BILL: This is like a ghost town.
JANE: You don't suppose there are any ghosts here, do you?
BILL: Don't be silly. There are no such things as ghosts . . .

(A low moan is heard from behind the counter)

JANE: I thought you said there were no such things as ghosts!
BILL: There aren't.
JANE: Then, what was that sound?
BILL: I don't know, but maybe I'd better find out . . .

(Advances to counter)

BILL: *(haltingly)* Co . . co . . come out of there, whoever you are.

(A head slowly begins to appear behind the counter. Bill retreats to where Jane is standing. The figure behind the counter rises and turns out to be Dowdy Dan.)

BILL: Who are you?
DAN: They call me Dowdy Dan, the hobo.
JANE: *(hesitatingly)* Well . . . I guess we're glad to meet you, but are you the only person in town?
DAN: Not exactly. The others are all at the dance in the village square, celebrating Rock Candy Day.

BILL:	What's that?
DAN:	It's a holiday, like National Sweet Tooth Day. Here come some of the people now.

(Enter Bert, Sally, Sam, and villagers, singing. Dowdy Dan hides behind Bill and Jane.)

(Song: "The Village Square," p. 78.)

SAM:	Howdy, folks. What can I do for you?
BILL:	Nothing, really. We were just passing through and thought we'd stop for a minute.
SAM:	Who's that behind you. Dowdy Dan! What are you doing here? We've been looking for you to help us celebrate.
DAN:	Just came to get some victuals, Sam.
SAM:	What do you plan to use for money?
DAN:	Oh, I've got money now. Just finished helping Farmer Brown clear up the north 40. Trouble is, he wanted to pay me in hay and I don't have much use for hay since Tururu died.
JANE:	Who is Tururu?
SALLY:	Tururu was Dowdy Dan's donkey.
JANE:	What happened to him?

(Dowdy Dan sings, "Lament for a Donkey," p. 15. At the conclusion, Grandma Grunts enters, carrying a basket of apples.)

SAM:	How's the apple business, Grandma?
GRANDMA:	Not too good, Sam. Seems like everybody's buying candy today 'stead of my apples.
JANE:	Are they cooking apples or eating apples, ma'am?
GRANDMA:	All kinds, girl. Listen, and I'll tell you.

(Grandma Grunts sings, "Buy My Apples," p. 86.)

BILL:	They sound awfully good. I'll take a red one and a green one.

(Jane starts to whistle the tune of "Buy My Apples." Grandma Grunts interrupts her.)

GRANDMA:	Don't do that, girl.
JANE:	Do what?
GRANDMA:	Whistle like that.
JANE:	Why not?

124

GRANDMA:	*(Joined by Sam)* Because boys can whistle—but girls should sing!
	(All join in singing, "Grandma Grunts," p. 148.)
BILL:	Well, we know you grow apples and all sorts of food on your farms. What else do you do in the country?
BERT:	We raise animals.
BILL:	What kinds?
BERT:	All kinds. Cows, pigs, chickens, sheep . . .
BILL:	What do you do with the sheep?
BILL:	We shear them for their wool.
JANE:	Doesn't it hurt them?
BERT:	Not a bit.
	(Bert sings, "Click, Go the Shears!", p. 42. During the song, three dairy maids enter.)
JANE:	Well, that's fine if you're a boy. But what do girls do in the country?
SALLY:	Lots of things. We have sewing bees, and taffy pulls, and we go on picnics . . .
JANE:	What do these girls do?
MAIDS:	We're the dairy maids.
	(The girls sing, "Dairy Maids," p. 96.)
SAM:	Well, now you've met some of us country folk . . .
GRANDMA:	And you 've learned about whistling . . .
DAN:	And my donkey . . .
MAIDS:	And churning . . .
JANE:	It's all been very interesting. But I'd like to know more about how you celebrate Rock Candy Day.
SAM:	Dan's the one to tell you about it. Why don't you, Dan? Then we'll all go back to the square and dance some more.

(Led by Dan, all sing "Big Rock Candy Mountain," p. 84. Exit at end.)

CURTAIN

Solveig's Song

FROM "PEER GYNT"
WORDS BY H. G. TREBILCOX
MUSIC BY EDVARD GRIEG

Andante

Though win - ter fades a - way   And the   soft, spring breez - es   die,

The __ soft, spring breez - es   die. _____   Though sum - mer

dis - ap - pears   And the   au - tumn   days   go   by,

The __ au - tumn days go by, _____   I   know the day will

dawn   When I'll   see   you a - gain,   I   know the day will

dawn. And on that hap - py morn - ing My cares will

all be gone, My cares will all be gone.

Peer Gynt, Suite No. 1

BY EDVARD GRIEG

A "suite" is a collection of short pieces. They may be various dances or, as in the "Peer Gynt Suite," several pieces of *incidental music*. Incidental music is written to accompany a stage play. The play, "Peer Gynt," was written by Ibsen, a famous Norwegian dramatist. Grieg wrote music to heighten the dramatic effect of several scenes in the play.

Peer has many adventures. One of them leads him to "The Hall of the Mountain King," where the dwarfs who live in a mountain cavern perform an exciting dance.

Here is the melody of this dance.

Another scene finds Peer watching a sunrise. This music is called "Morning."

Here is the melody.

You would expect these two pieces to be quite different.
How does Grieg give them contrast?

Wonderful Copenhagen

FROM "HANS CHRISTIAN ANDERSEN"
WORDS AND MUSIC BY FRANK LOESSER

Wistfully

I sail up the Skag-ge-rak, and sail down the Kat-te-gat

Through the har - bor and up to the quay, And there she stands,

wait - ing for me, With a wel - come so warm and so gay. ___

Refrain

Won - der - ful, won - der - ful Co - pen - ha - gen,

friend - ly old girl of a town, ___ With her har - bor light,

that she wears at night, like a gold - en, gold - en crown. __

Oh, won - der -ful, won - der-ful Co - pen - ha - gen,

salt - y old queen of the sea, __ Once I sailed a - way,

but I'm home to - day, Sing - ing Co - pen - ha - gen,

won - der -ful, won - der -ful Co - pen - ha - gen for me. __

POETRY AND MUSIC

A Cradle Hymn

WORDS BY ISAAC WATTS
MUSIC BY JOHANN SEBASTIAN BACH

Hush, my dear, lie still and slum - ber,

Ho - ly an - gels guard thy bed.

Heav'n - ly bless - ings with - out num - ber

gen - tly fall - ing on thy head.

2. How much better thou'rt attended
    Than the Son of God could be,
    When from heaven He descended
    And became a child like thee.

3. Mayest thou like to know and fear Him,
    Trust and love Him all thy days,
    Then go dwell forever near Him
    See His face and sing His praise.

130

Give Us This Day Our Daily Bread

WORDS AND MUSIC
BY STEPHEN FOSTER

Reverently

1. Fa - ther of Love, Fa - ther of Love,
2. Hum - bly we pray, hum - bly we pray,

Send down Thy bless - ings on ____ each head;
Words that our Lord ____ Re - deem - er said;

Shield us from pride while here we bide, }
Trust - ful and weak, hum - bly we speak, }

Give us, this day, ____ our dai - ly bread.

Give us, this day, our dai - ly bread.

Many of Stephen Foster's songs are ballads which use either a romantic or sentimental text. Some of his most famous songs are "Jeanie with the Light Brown Hair," "Beautiful Dreamer," "Oh, Susanna," "Old Folks at Home," and "Old Dog Tray." This is one of Foster's few sacred songs. It should be sung smoothly and quietly to emphasize the reverent mood.

Marching Song

WORDS BY ROBERT LOUIS STEVENSON
MUSIC BY HARRY R. WILSON

Stevenson wrote many
poems just for children.

Steadily

Bring a comb and play up - on it! March-ing, here we come!

Wil - lie cocks his high - land bon - net, John - nie beats the drum.

Mar - y Jane com - mands the par - ty, Pet - er leads the rear;

Feet in time, a - lert and heart - y, Each a Gren - a - dier!

All in the most mar - tial man - ner, March-ing dou - ble quick;

While the nap - kin, like a ban - ner, Waves up - on the stick!

Can you make up an introduction and coda for this song? To help keep the rhythm steady, you might tap quarter note patterns in the measures which use notes of longer time value.

132

Here's e - nough of fame and pil - lage, Great com - mand-er Jane!

Now that we've been 'round the vil - lage, Let's go home a - gain! —

Oh, Sailor, Come Ashore

WORDS BY CHRISTINA ROSSETTI
MUSIC BY ARTHUR FRACKENPOHL

Wistfully

Oh, sail - or, come a - shore, What have you brought for me?

Red cor - al, white cor - al, Cor - al from the sea.

2. I did not pluck it from the ground,
   Nor pluck it from a tree;
   Feeble insects made it in the
   Stormy, stormy sea.

Where Go the Boats?

WORDS BY ROBERT LOUIS STEVENSON
MUSIC BY ARTHUR FRACKENPOHL

This fanciful poem about water
uses many descriptive words.

Gracefully

1. Dark brown is   the riv - er, _____   Gold - en is _ the sand. _
2. On   goes ___   the riv - er, _ And out ___ past _ the mill; _

It   flows a - long for - ev - er _ With trees on ei - ther hand. _
A - way ___ down the val - ley, _ A - way ___ down the hill. _ A -

Green leaves ___ a - float-ing, _____   Cas - tles of __ the foam.
way   down ___ the riv - er, ___   A   hun - dred miles _ or   more,

Boats of mine   a - boat-ing, _____   When will all come home?
Oth - er lit - tle chil-dren ___ Shall bring my boats a - shore.

Do, Boatman, Do

This poem is also about water, but
it is simple, direct, and tells a story.

WORDS BY CHRISTINA ROSSETTI
MUSIC BY ELIZABETH ELSBREE

Lightly

"Fer - ry me a - cross the wa - ter, Do, boat - man, do."

"If you've a pen - ny in your purse, I'll fer - ry you."

"I have a pen - ny in my purse, And my eyes are blue,

So fer - ry me a - cross the wat - er, Do, boat - man, do!"

"Step in - to my fer - ry boat, Be they black or blue,

And for the pen - ny in your purse, I'll fer - ry you."

The Lord My Pasture Shall Prepare

PARAPHRASE OF PSALM 23
BY JOSEPH ADDISON
ARAB MELODY

Reverently

1. The Lord my pas - ture shall pre - pare, And feed me with a
2. And when I faint on moun-tain trail, Or on hot sands my

shep-herd's _ care; His pres - ence shall my wants sup - ply, And
spir - its __ fail, To fer - tile vales and dew - y meads, My

guard me with a watch-ful _ eye; My noon - day walks He
wear - y wan - d'ring steps He _ leads; Where peace-ful riv - ers,

shall at - tend, And all my mid - night hours de - fend. ____
soft and slow, A - mid the ver - dant land-scape _ flow. ____

3. Although in darkest paths I tread,
   Of unknown perils feel no dread;
   My steadfast heart shall feel no ill,
   For Thou, O Lord, art with me still;
   Thy friendly crook shall give me aid,
   And gently guide me through the shade.

The Swallow

WORDS BY CHRISTINA ROSSETTI
MUSIC BY E. J. HERMANN

Liltingly

Fly a - way, fly a - way, o - ver the sea,

Sun - lov - ing swal - low, for sum - mer is done.

Come a - gain, come a - gain, Come back to me,

Bring - ing the sum - mer and bring - ing the sun.

The Duck and the Kangaroo

WORDS BY EDWARD LEAR
MUSIC BY PAUL KAPP

Steadily

1. Said the Duck to the Kan - ga - roo, ___ "Good gra - cious,
2. "Please ___ give me a ride on your back," ___ Said the Duck to the

how you hop, ___ O - ver the fields and the
Kan - ga - roo, ___ "I would sit ___ quite still and say

wa - ter, too, As if you would nev - er stop; ___ My
noth - ing but 'Quack' The whole of the long day through; ___ And we'd

life is a bore in this nas - ty pond And I
go to the Dee and the Jel - ly Bo Lee,

long to go out in the world be - yond, I ___ wish I could
O - ver the land ___ and o - ver the sea; Please ___ take me for a

hop like you!" ___ Said the Duck to the Kan - ga - roo. ___
ride, Oh, do!" ___ Said the Duck to the Kan - ga - roo. ___

Published by General Music Publishing Co.
Reprinted by permission of the author.

3. Said the Kangaroo to the Duck,
   "This requires some little reflection;
   Perhaps on the whole it might bring me luck,
   And there seems but one objection,
   Which is, if you'll let me speak so bold,
   Your feet are unpleasantly wet and cold,
   And would probably give me the roo-
   Matiz!" said the Kangaroo.

4. Said the Duck, "As I sat on the rocks,
   I have thought that over completely,
   And I bought four pairs of worsted socks
   Which fit my web-feet neatly.
   And to keep out the cold I've bought a cloak,
   And every day a cigar I'll smoke,
   All to follow my own dear true
   Love of a Kangaroo."

5. Said the Kangaroo, "I'm ready!
   All in the moonlight pale;
   But to balance me well, dear Duck, sit steady!
   And quite at the end of my tail!"
   So away they went with a hop and a bound,
   And they hopped the whole world three times round;
   And who so happy—oh, who,
   As the Duck and the Kangaroo?

CREATING MUSIC

The song below is called "The Weather Vane." The main tune is on the upper staff. On the lower staff is another tune which can be played on the bells or sung at the same time the main tune is sung. This little tune has three different tones, which are repeated measure by measure. This is called an *ostinato*.

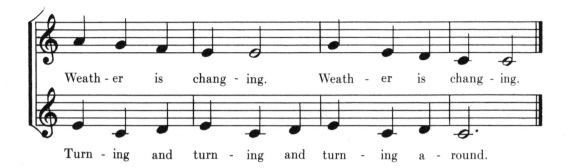

Weath - er   is   chang - ing.   Weath - er   is   chang - ing.

Turn - ing   and   turn - ing   and   turn - ing   a - round.

Here are rhythm patterns for two parts. Clap each part separately, then half of the class may clap the top rhythm while the other half claps the lower one.

These rhythms may also be clapped as a two-part round. Everyone claps both lines through once. Part II enters on line 1 as Part I begins line 2.

It is also fun to play rhythms on instruments. In the "Percussion Fantasy" that follows, each group of instruments plays its rhythm in turn. Then, as the cymbals finish their rhythm, each group plays its own rhythm *at the same time*.

The Pentatonic Scale

There are five tones in the pentatonic scale. Many primitive peoples have used it in their music. The following American Indian song is built on a pentatonic scale. You can sing this song, play it on bells or recorder or song flute, and add a drum accompaniment if you wish.

Hi yo, hi yo ip see nee yah, hi yo; Hi yo ip see

nee — yah, hi — yo; Hi yo ip see nee yah, hi — yo;

Hi yo ip see nee yah, hi — yo. Hi yo hi!

This is a pentatonic scale:

Played on white keys:

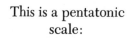

Played on black keys:

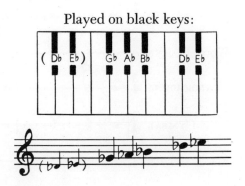

142

Using the tones of the pentatonic scale, make up a tune for the words of the poem that appears below.

SOARING BIRD

Fly, fly, high in the sky,
After the rain and the thunder.
Sing, sing, let your song ring,
Over the rainbow and under.

You have learned that when we listen to the rhythm of the words, they tell us what to do. Poetry, like music, has accents and rhythm. Usually there is a steady beat which determines the meter. To find the beat, listen for the accents.

Beat a drum to this measure | ♩ ♩ ♩ | and say the words in this rhythm:

Words that are strongly rhythmic often suggest a melody as we say them aloud. When you have sung your melody for these words, you will want to write it in your music notebook so you can remember it. It is easy to find the pentatonic scale on the piano if you play the pitches on the black keys. Play your melody on the black keys; then write it, using the diagram on the opposite page.

An *ostinato* may be spoken as well as sung. Here are two that may be repeated over and over again as the poem is spoken or sung. Use them also to make a coda and an introduction.

143

Mood and Music

You have learned that words, spoken rhythmically, may suggest a tune. It is also true that a tune tells you what kind of words suit it best, when you listen carefully. Some tunes are gay; some march along; others are sad. This is called the *mood* of the music.

The following song needs two more lines of poetry. What kind of words are needed?

When   I   see   the   stars   on   high,

In   the   dark - ness   of   night. _____

Is this a gay or quiet mood? Should the song by sung quickly or slowly? As you sing the tune with "loo," which way sounds best? Look at the *tempo marks* in your music book, in the left-hand corner above the songs, and choose one you think might be suitable for this song.

A song with short, fast notes is generally about something happy and active. One with many long, slow notes is usually thoughtful and about quieter things.

Melodies may move smoothly by scale steps, skip about, or use repeated notes. Each suggests different kinds of words. Would the above melody make a good song about a clown or a jumping jack?

144

Sing the tune again and listen to the rise and fall of each of the phrases. Can you hear the last phrase rising to tell of some quietly joyful thing?

Now that the music has suggested appropriate words, write the lines of poetry needed. Remember that accented words and syllables should follow bar lines. Also that the third line should rhyme with "high," and the last line with "night."

Below is a short melody that has no words at all. It does have a tempo mark telling you that the song should be sung quickly and brightly. Sing this tune over and over with "loo," until you are familiar with it.

What is the mood of this tune? Contrast it with the song on the opposite page. Is this daytime or nighttime music? The night song has flowing phrases and many long notes. This song has short, quick notes. Its melody is broken with rests. There are short figures that repeat, giving snap to the tune.

The meter signature is different, too. Have you noticed that many songs that suggest motion are written in 4/4 meter? Does this tune in 4/4 meter make you think of moving to it? If so, how would you move?

The words you make up for this tune might begin with "We like to march," or "Let's do a dance," or "We're jumping rope." Someone might like to start with "Just hear us sing" and go on to describe what kind of song this is.

Have you noticed that songs with repeated figures often have repeated words? Your words might start, "I like to sing, I like to sing, I like to sing a happy tune."

When you have made up your words, copy this music in your notebook, with your words in the proper place. Then put "Words by ...." above your song.

145

Using Minor Keys

Songs written in minor keys have a mood and color all their own. Review some of the minor songs you have learned and listen carefully to them. A sad song may sound sadder when written in minor than one in a major key. However, minor songs are not always sad. Many are bright and gay. Try to find an example of a gay song in minor.

Here is a minor melody without words. It moves quickly. What kind of mood is it? Sing it with "loo" until you know the tune, then choose your words to fit the music.

Complete the following minor melody. All the words are given. A minor key seems to fit a song about the cruel North wind and the chilling cold of a large snowfall.

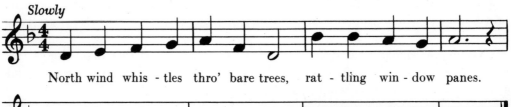

North wind whis - tles thro' bare trees, rat - tling win - dow panes.

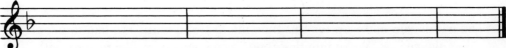

Snow drifts high - er than my knees cov - ver streets and lanes.

Look for other short poems that express a definite mood. Try to make up tunes for them expressing this mood. Try writing two tunes for the same words, one in major, one in minor. Compare them and see which better expresses the mood of the words. Copy your songs in your notebook and keep adding those you write at home. Here are some titles for a song: "Holidays," "Pets," "Blast Off," "A Lullaby."

FUN AND NONSENSE

The Little Crocodile

WORDS BY LEWIS CARROLL
MUSIC BY DAVID POLLOCK

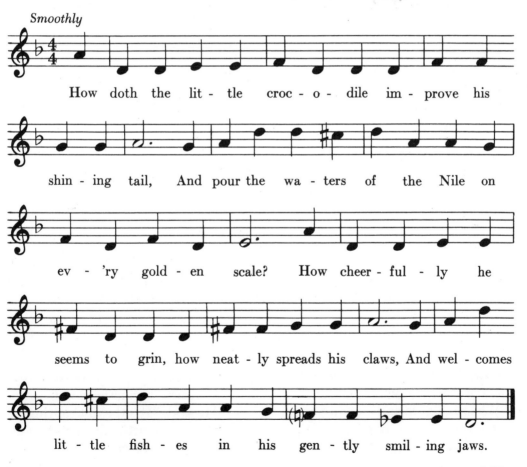

Smoothly

How doth the lit - tle croc - o - dile im - prove his

shin - ing tail, And pour the wa - ters of the Nile on

ev - 'ry gold - en scale? How cheer - ful - ly he

seems to grin, how neat - ly spreads his claws, And wel - comes

lit - tle fish - es in his gen - tly smil - ing jaws.

147

Grandma Grunts

TRADITIONAL

After you have learned the song,
you might enjoy whistling
the lower voice part.

Brightly
(*Whistle*)

1. Grand - ma Grunts said a fun - ny thing, "Boys can
2. Boys can whis - tle, of course they may, Boys can

whis - tle, but girls must sing." That was what I
whis - tle the live - long day. Can't girls whis - tle,

heard her say, 'Twas no long - er than yes - ter - day. ⎫
too, pray tell? If they man - age to do it well! ⎭

Refrain (*Whistle*)

Boys can whis-tle, Girls must sing, Tra la la la la.

3. Grandma Grunts said it wouldn't do,
   Gave a very good reason, too,
   Whistling girls and crowing hens
   Always come to some bad ends.
      (*Refrain*)

4. Asked my papa the reason why
   Girls can't whistle as well as I,
   He said, "It's the nat'ral thing
   Boys to whistle and girls to sing."
      (*Refrain*)

148

One, Two, Three, Four

WORDS ADAPTED
BY CLAUDIA REGEN
MUSIC BY J. ALAU

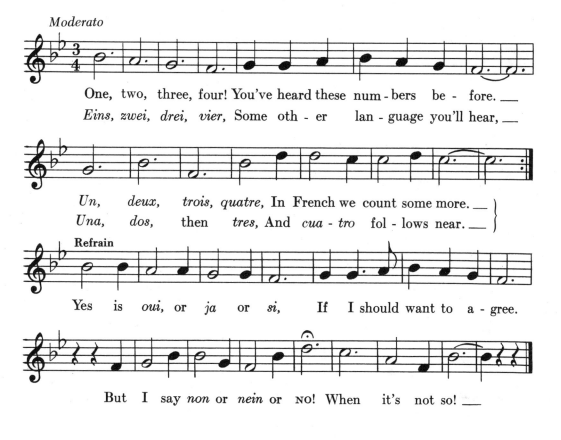

Moderato

One, two, three, four! You've heard these num - bers be - fore. __
Eins, zwei, drei, vier, Some oth - er lan - guage you'll hear, __

Un, deux, trois, quatre, In French we count some more. __
Una, dos, then tres, And *cua - tro* fol - lows near. __

Refrain

Yes is *oui,* or *ja* or *si,* If I should want to a - gree.

But I say *non* or *nein* or NO! When it's not so! __

Here are some numbers in four different
languages that you can use in this song.

Latin		Italian		Swedish		Dutch	
one	— **unus**	one	— **uno**	one	— **ett**	one	— **een**
two	— **duo**	two	— **due**	two	— **tva**	two	— **twee**
three	— **tres**	three	— **tre**	three	— **tre**	three	— **drie**
four	— **quattuor**	four	— **quattro**	four	— **fyra**	four	— **vier**

Jig Along Home

WORDS AND MUSIC
BY WOODY GUTHRIE

There are two beats in each measure
of this song. Clap your hands on each
beat to feel the swing of the music.

Gaily

1. I went to a dance and the an - i - mals came,
2. The fish did a dance to the fish - ing ___ reel,

The jay - bird danced with horse - shoes on,
The lob - ster danced on the pea - cock's tail,

The grass - hop - per danced till he fell on the floor,
The ba - boon ___ danced with the ris - ing ___ moon,

Jig a - long, jig a - long, jig a - long home.

Refrain

Jig, jig a - jig, jig a - jig a - long home.

Jig, jig a - jig, jig a - jig a - long home.

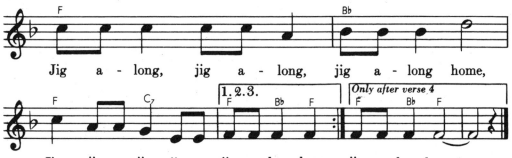

Jig a - long, jig a - long, jig a - long home,

1. 2. 3.
F   Bb   F

Only after verse 4
F   Bb   F

Jig, jig a - jig, jig a - jig a - long home. jig a - long home! —

3.   Mama rat took off her hat,
         Shook the house with the old tom cat,
         The alligator beat his tail on the drum,
         Jig along, jig along, jig along home.
                (Refrain)

4.   The nails flew loose and the floor broke down,
         Everybody danced around and around,
         The house came down, the crowd went home,
         Jig along, jig along, jig along home.
                (Refrain)

The Letter "E" Song

WORDS BY YVONNE CARR
FRENCH FOLK TUNE

Can you think of other words in which an "e" makes a difference? The "e" need not come at the end of the word. For example, **bat** and **beat**.

Vigorously

1. Take the "e" from "ate" and I'm left with "at,"
2. Add an "e" to "mat" and I have a "mate,"

Take the "e" from "rate" and I'm left with "rat,"
Add an "e" to "pat" and I have a "pate,"

And if the "e" is gone from "fate," don't you see
But if I add an "e" to "be," you will see,

I would be left with on - ly "fat," you'll a - gree.}
I'll have a bus - y lit - tle "bee," you'll a - gree.}

Oh my, what a change, Oh my, what a change,

How dif - f'rent it can be, Oh my, what a change,

Oh my, what a change To spell with - out an "e"!
add an - oth - er "e"!

Animal Song

Can you make up other verses
using different animals?

WORDS AND MUSIC
BY EMELYN E. GARDNER

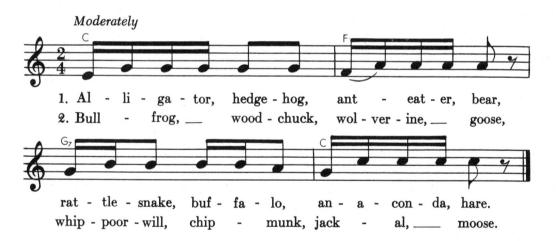

1. Al - li - ga - tor, hedge - hog, ant - eat - er, bear,
2. Bull - frog, ___ wood - chuck, wol - ver - ine, ___ goose,

rat - tle - snake, buf - fa - lo, an - a - con - da, hare.
whip - poor - will, chip - munk, jack - al, ___ moose.

3. Mud turtle, whale, glow-worm, bat,
   Salamander, snail, and Maltese cat.

4. Polecat, dog, wild otter, rat,
   Pelican, hog, dodo, and bat.

5. House rat, toe rat, white bear, doe,
   Chickadee, peacock, bobolink, and crow.

Shule, Shule

OZARK FOLK SONG

Rhythmically

I went to the riv-er and I could-n't get a-cross,

I paid five dol-lars for an old gray horse,

I rode him in and he could-n't swim.

Shul-ey, shul-ey, shal-ly, wig-gle round,

Shule, shule, shal-ly wig-gle round, Shol-ey ank-a

shol-ey ank and shol-ey pop-pa kew,

154

Cross out a wig - gle and a who jaw lang,

Sick a jid - dle in a ban - jo land.

Kookaburra

AUSTRALIAN ROUND

Briskly

Koo - ka - bur - ra sits on an old gum tree, ___ Mer - ry,

mer - ry king of the bush is he, ___ Laugh, koo - ka -

bur - ra, Laugh, koo - ka - bur - ra, Gay your life must be.

155

I've Been to Haarlem

AMERICAN FOLK SONG

Haarlem is one of the largest
cities in the Netherlands.

Rhythmically

I've been to Haar - lem, I've been to Do - ver, I've trav- eled

this wide world all o - ver, O - ver, o - ver, three times o - ver,

Find me an - oth - er ship when this trip is o - ver.

Refrain

Sail - ing east, sail - ing west, sail - ing o - ver the o - cean,

Bet - ter watch out when the boat be - gins to rock,

Or you'll lose your girl in the o - cean.

Sway back and forth, twice in each measure, to feel the swing of the music.
You can also imitate the rolling motion of a ship in this way.

Eleven Little Froggies

WORDS AND MUSIC
BY JOSEF MARAIS

Gaily

1. E - lev - en lit - tle frog - gies lived to - geth - er
2. They shiv - ered un - der - neath the ice, And then the
3. The love - ly spring - time weath - er came, the frogs came

in a creek. In win - ter when the wa - ter
young - est said: "That night - in - gale is sing - ing
out to sing, And ev - 'ry night those 'lev - en

froze, the frog - gies felt so weak, They did - n't croak, they
in the tree a - bove our head. I'm sick of lis - t'ning
frog - gies croaked the same old thing. The night - in - gale is

did - n't sing, they did - n't e - ven squeak.) 1.2. E - lev - en
to his song, I wish he'd shut his beak!") 3. I hope those
beau - ti - ful, He's mod - est and he's meek;

lit - tle frog - gies lived to - geth - er in a creek.___
stuck - up frogs go back in - to their fro - zen creek. ___

There Was an Old Woman

AMERICAN FOLK SONG

Easily

1. There was an old wom-an who swal-lowed a fly, And
I don't know why she swal-lowed a fly, Per-haps she'll die.

2. There was an old wom-an who swal-lowed a spi-der That
3. There was an old wom-an who swal-lowed a bird,___

wig-gled and jig-gled and tick-led in-side her,
How___ ab-surd ___ to swal-low a bird, ___

Verses accumulate

2. She swal-lowed a spi-der to swal-low a fly,
3. {She swal-lowed a bird ___
   to swal-low a spi-der to swal-low a fly,} And

I don't know why she swal-lowed a fly, Per-haps she'll die.

4. There was an old woman who swallowed a cat;
Imagine that—to swallow a cat.
She swallowed a cat—to swallow a bird—to swallow a spider—
to swallow a fly, And I don't know why she swallowed a fly,
Perhaps she'll die.

5. There was an old woman who swallowed a dog;
What a hog to swallow a dog.
She swallowed a dog—to swallow a cat—to swallow a bird—
to swallow a spider—to swallow a fly,
And I don't know why she swallowed a fly,
Perhaps she'll die.

6. There was an old woman who swallowed a goat;
Just opened her throat and swallowed a goat.
She swallowed a goat—to swallow a dog—to swallow a cat—
to swallow a bird—to swallow a spider—to swallow a fly,
And I don't know why she swallowed a fly,
Perhaps she'll die.

7. There was an old woman who swallowed a cow;
I don't know how she swallowed a cow.
She swallowed a cow—to swallow a goat—to swallow a dog—
to swallow a cat—to swallow a bird—to swallow a spider—
to swallow a fly, And I don't know why she swallowed a fly,
Perhaps she'll die.

8. There was an old wom - an who swal - lowed a horse;

She's dead of course.

Kemo Kimo

TENNESSEE MOUNTAIN SONG

The frog who courts a mouse is a
favorite subject of many folk songs.

Steadily

1. There was a frog lived in a spring,
2. Says he, "Miss Mouse are you with - in?"

Sing song, Kit - ty, can't you Ki - me - o?

He went down the road, Mous - ie's bell to ring,
"Yes, yes, Oh, kind sir, here I sit and spin,"

Sing song, Kit - ty, can't you Ki - me - o?

Refrain

Ke - mo Ki - mo dee ro art, Me - he me - hi Me -

hum - drum pen - ny win - kle, Tit, tat, pit - ty pat,

blue - eyed pus - sy   cat,   Sing   song Kit - ty, can't you Ki - me - o?

3.   He took Miss Mousie on his knee,
     Sing song, Kitty, can't you Kimeo?
     And said, "Dear Miss Mouse will you marry me?"
     Sing song, Kitty, can't you Kimeo?
          (Refrain)

4.   Says she, "Oh, what a nice young man!"
     Sing song, Kitty, can't you Kimeo?
     "I'll do it today if I find I can."
     Sing song, Kitty, can't you Kimeo?
          (Refrain)

Finale

FROM "CARNIVAL OF ANIMALS"
BY CAMILLE SAINT-SAENS

In the "Carnival of the Animals," Saint-Saens wrote musical pictures of many different animals. He wrote the music to imitate either the sound or the movement of the animals. Among the animals are turtles, elephants, fish, and a lion.

Here is one of the themes from the "Finale."
What animals do you think it represents?

In the "Finale" of the suite, many of the animals appear again as though they were taking a bow. Can you hear the hee-haw of the donkey, the clucking hens, the hopping kangaroo, or the roaring lion? You should be able to hear in the music the pianist who only practises scales all day long.

Throw It Out the Window

TRADITIONAL

Cheerfully

1. Sim - ple Si - mon met ___ a pie - man,
2. Lit - tle Miss Muf - fet sat on a tuf - fet,
3. Old ___ King Cole was a mer - ry old soul, A

Go - ing to the fair, ___ Said Sim - ple Si - mon
Eat - ing her curds and whey! ___ A - long came a spi - der and
mer - ry old soul was he. ___ He called for his pipe and he

to ___ the pie - man, "Throw it out the win - dow! ___
sat down be - side her; She threw him out the win - dow! ___
called for his bowl; ___ And threw them out the win - dow! ___

Oh, throw it out the win - dow." ___
The win - dow, ___ the win - dow, ___ She threw him out the win - dow. ___
He threw them out the win - dow. ___

You can make up additional verses using Mother Goose rhymes. Try using "Little Jack Horner," "Rub-A-Dub-Dub," or "Hey, Diddle, Diddle." You will have to change the last line of each poem. For example, in "Little Jack Horner," you might have:

He put in his thumb
And pulled out a plum,
And threw it out the window.

The Ring and the Box

WORDS ADAPTED
BY MARTHA HARRIS
PHILIPPINE MELODY

Wistfully

BOYS: 1. I will give you a ring, One that's pret - ty and rare,
GIRLS: 2. I will give you a box, One that's filled to the brim,
ALL: 3. A - tin cu pung sing - sing Me - tong yang tim - pu - can,

It will make your heart sing, It will show you I care.
It will be with- out locks, And will make your head swim.
A - ma - na - que - i - ti, Qng in - oung i - ba - tan.

GIRLS: For the ring I did crave, And my friends wished me well,
BOYS: Oh, the box meant a lot, And I smiled through my tears,
ALL: *Sang - can queng si - ni - nup, Qng me - tung a - ca - ban,*

But the ring that you gave was the ring of a bell!
But the box that I got was a box on the ears!
Me - wa - la ya i - ti, E - cu ca - ma - la - yan.

You might make up additional verses for this song as well. Try to think of phrases with a catch word in them, such as . . .

a **lock** of your hair,
the **lace** of your shoe,
the **band** of a watch,
a **coat** of blue paint.

SONGS FOR SPECIAL DAYS

The Star-Spangled Banner

WORDS BY FRANCIS SCOTT KEY
MUSIC BY JOHN STAFFORD SMITH

Vigorously

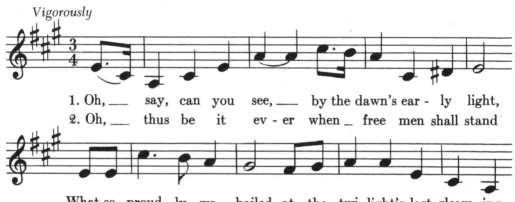

1. Oh, ___ say, can you see, ___ by the dawn's ear - ly light,
2. Oh, ___ thus be it ev - er when ___ free men shall stand

What so proud - ly we hailed at the twi - light's last gleam - ing,
Be - tween their loved homes and the war's des - o - la - tion,

Whose broad stripes and bright stars, through the per - il - ous fight,
Blessed with vic - t'ry and peace, may the heav'n res - cued land

O'er the ram - parts we watched were so gal - lant - ly stream - ing?
Praise the pow'r that hath made and pre - served us a na - tion.

And the rock - ets' red glare, the bombs burst - ing in air,
Then — con - quer we must, when our cause it is just,

Gave proof through the night that our flag was still there;
And this be our mot - to, "In God is our trust!"

Refrain

Oh, say, does that — Star - span - gled Ban - ner — yet — wave —
And the Star - span-gled — Ban - ner in tri-umph — shall — wave —

O'er the land — of the free and the home of the brave?
O'er the land — of the free and the home of the brave!

Halloween Song

WORDS AND MUSIC
BY GEORGE K. EVANS

The eerie mood of this song is
emphasized by the minor melody.

Distinctly

Elves and gob - lins prowl - ing, Witch - es rid - ing on air,

Cats yowl - ing, Ghosts howl - ing, Mon - sters are ev - 'ry - where.

Skel - e - tons danc - ing clack, click, clack,

Grue - some fac - es are seen;

If this scares you half to death,

It's be-cause it's Hal - low - een! *(Shriek)*

On the First Thanksgiving Day

TRADITIONAL

Reverently

On the first Thanks - giv - ing Day,
Thanked the Lord for sun and rain,

Pil - grims went to church to pray,
Thanked Him for the fields of grain.

Now Thanks - giv - ing comes a - gain,

Praise the Lord as they did then,

Thank Him for the sun and rain,

Thank Him for the fields of grain.

All be Brothers, Hallelu

WORDS BY ROLLA FOLEY
ARAB MELODY

The accents show you which
words are to be stressed.

Rhythmically

Refrain

All　　be broth - ers,　bound　to - geth - er,
Bound　to - geth - er,　like　the sheaves of grain,

Fine

All　　　be broth - ers,　Hal - le - lu,
To　　the Lord give thanks a - new.

Verse

1. Joy - ous - ly we greet this Har - vest Tide,
2. All　　be broth - ers,　bound　to - geth - er,
3. Figs　are gath - ered,　oil　is flow - ing,

Broth - ers all,　u - nit - ed is our love.
Like　the gold - en grain we're new - ly bound.
Bins　are filled to brim with har - vest store.

Bind - ing the grain, we raise Hearts full of thank - ful praise
Though struck by sick - le thrust, Still in our God we trust,
Si - lent in prayer we stand, Thanks for our fruit - ful land,

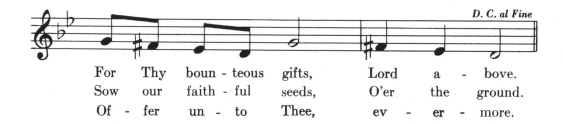

For Thy boun - teous gifts, Lord a - bove.
Sow our faith - ful seeds, O'er the ground.
Of - fer un - to Thee, ev - er - more.

Father, We Thank Thee

WORDS BY RALPH WALDO EMERSON
MUSIC BY RAYMOND ELLIOTT

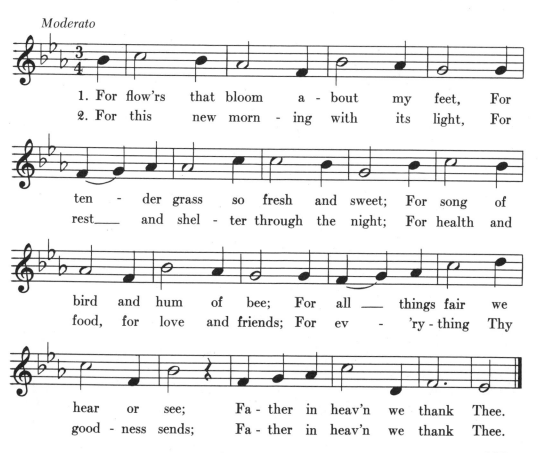

Moderato

1. For flow'rs that bloom a - bout my feet, For
2. For this new morn - ing with its light, For

ten - der grass so fresh and sweet; For song of
rest___ and shel - ter through the night; For health and

bird and hum of bee; For all ___ things fair we
food, for love and friends; For ev - 'ry - thing Thy

hear or see; Fa - ther in heav'n we thank Thee.
good - ness sends; Fa - ther in heav'n we thank Thee.

O Hanukah

WORDS BY RUSSELL NORMAN
HEBREW SONG

Moderately

Come, see the can - dles burn-ing, See them burn - ing so bright-ly,

See how each flame dan - ces Ev - er so light - ly,

1.   2.

Ev - 'ry heart is gay when it's Ha - nu - kah time,
Hap - py hol - i - day, for it's Ha - nu - kah time;

See the can - dles burn - ing, See the can - dles burn - ing,

Each can - dle re - call - ing the

See the can - dles burn - ing;

deeds of the brave Mac - ca - bees,

Ah, _____ Ah, _____

Raise ev - 'ry voice, Let each spir - it re - joice,⟩ Cel - e -
Dance and be gay, throw all sor - row a - way,⟩

1.

Ah, _____ See the can - dles burn - ing,

brate, for it's Ha - nu - kah time,

2.

Ah, _____ See the can - dles burn.

brate, for it's Ha - nu - kah time.

Silent Night

WORDS BY JOSEPH MOHR
MUSIC BY FRANZ GRUBER

This is one of the most famous and best-loved of all Christmas carols.

1. Si - lent night, Ho - ly night, All is calm, all is bright,
2. Si - lent night, Ho - ly night, Shep-herds quake at the sight,

Round yon Vir - gin Moth - er and Child,
Glo - ries stream ___ from heav - en a - far,

Ho - ly In - fant so ten - der and mild;
Heav'n - ly hosts ___ sing "Al - le - lu - ia;"

Sleep in heav - en - ly peace, ___ Sleep ___ in heav - en - ly peace. ___
Christ the Sav - ior is born! ___ Christ ___ the Sav - ior is born! ___

3. Silent night, Holy night,
Son of God, love's pure light,
Radiant beams from Thy holy face,
With the dawn of redeeming grace,
Jesus, Lord at Thy birth,
Jesus, Lord at Thy birth.

4. Silent night, Holy night,
Wondrous Star, lend thy light.
With the angels let us sing,
Alleluia to our King;
Christ the Savior is born,
Christ the Savior is born.

Coventry Carol

ENGLISH CAROL

The words "lully" and "lullay"
are contractions of "lullaby."

Tenderly

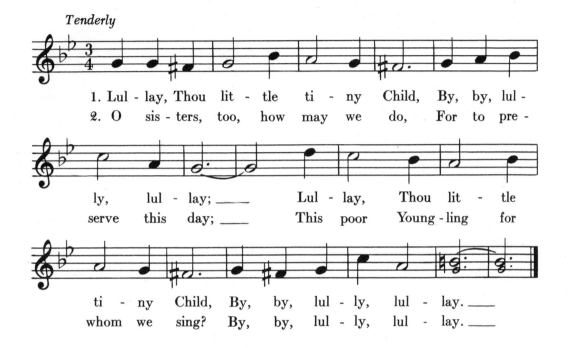

1. Lul - lay, Thou lit - tle ti - ny Child, By, by, lul -
2. O sis - ters, too, how may we do, For to pre -

ly, lul - lay; _____ Lul - lay, Thou lit - tle
serve this day; _____ This poor Young - ling for

ti - ny Child, By, by, lul - ly, lul - lay. _____
whom we sing? By, by, lul - ly, lul - lay. _____

3. Herod, the King, in his raging,
    Charged he hath this day;
    His men of might, in his own sight,
    All children-young, to slay.

4. Then woe is me, poor Child, for Thee,
    And ever mourn and say;
    For Thy parting nor say nor sing,
    By, by, lully, lullay.

As in many very old English songs, you will find that the melody may accent a syllable that
is normally unstressed. This will add to the charm and interest of the song.

The Friendly Beasts

TRADITIONAL ENGLISH CAROL
13th CENTURY NORMAN MELODY

Tenderly

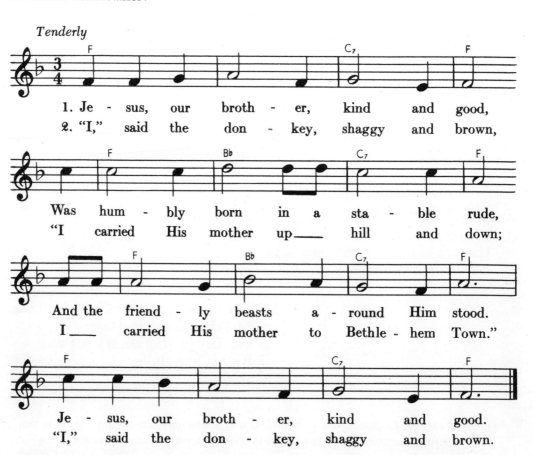

1. Je - sus, our broth - er, kind and good,
2. "I," said the don - key, shaggy and brown,

Was hum - bly born in a sta - ble rude,
"I carried His mother up___ hill and down;

And the friend - ly beasts a - round Him stood.
I___ carried His mother to Bethle - hem Town."

Je - sus, our broth - er, kind and good.
"I," said the don - key, shaggy and brown.

3. "I," said the cow all white and red,
   "I gave him my manger for his bed,
   I gave him my hay to pillow his head,"
   "I," said the cow, all white and red.

4. "I," said the sheep, with curly horn,
   "I gave him my wool for his blanket warm;
   He wore my coat on Christmas morn."
   "I," said the sheep with curly horn.

5. "I," said the dove from the rafters high,
   "Cooed him to sleep that he should not cry,
   We cooed him to sleep, my mate and I,"
   "I," said the dove from the rafters high.

6. Thus every beast by some good spell,
   In the stable dark was glad to tell
   Of the gift he gave Immanuel,
   The gift he gave Immanuel.

Go Tell it on the Mountain

SPIRITUAL

Moderately

1. When I was a seek - er, I sought both night and day,
2. He made me a watch - man up - on a cit - y wall,

I asked the Lord to help me, An' He showed me the way.
An' if I am a Chris - tian, I am the least of all.

Descant

Go, tell it on the moun - tain,

Go tell it on the moun - tain,

Go, Go, Go,

O - ver the hills and ev - 'ry - where, — Go tell it on the

Tell it on the moun - tain, Je - sus Christ _ is born.

moun - tain That Je - sus Christ _ is born.

The **chorale** is a special type of hymn.
One of the features of a chorale is
the **fermata** at the end of each phrase.

Beside Thy Manger

ADAPTED FROM MARTIN LUTHER
MUSIC BY JOHANN SEBASTIAN BACH

Smoothly

1. Be - side Thy man - ger here I stand, Dear Je - sus
2. With joy I gaze up - on Thy face. Thy glo - ry

Lord, and _ Sav - ior; A gift of love _ with -
and Thy _ splen - dor Are great - er than _ my

in my hand To thank Thee for Thy _ fa - vor.
heart can praise, And songs can fit - ly _ ren - der.

177

Lullaby

WORDS BY A. G. CORNER
MUSIC BY ROBERT V. BALLAGH

There are three phrases in this song.
Which two are exactly alike?

Tenderly

1. A babe lies in a cra - dle, A lit - tle
2. Who - so would rock the cra - dle Where lies the

babe so dear; With no - ble light He shin - eth,
gen - tle Child, A low - ly heart must lead ___ him,

As shines a mir - ror clear. Oh, sleep, my Child,
As Ma - ry pure and mild. Oh, sleep, my Child,

Only after verse 3

Oh, sleep, my Child.)
Oh, sleep, my Child. } Oh, sleep, my Child Di - vine.

3. Oh, Jesus, Babe beloved,
   Oh, Jesus, Babe divine.
   How mighty is Thy wond'rous love,
   Fill Thou this heart of mine.
   Oh, sleep, my Child, Oh, sleep, my Child.

Carol of the Birds

Listen to the melody of this song.
Is it in a major or minor key?

FRENCH CAROL

Joyfully

1. Whence comes this rush of wings a - far,
2. "Tell us, ye birds, why come ye here

Fol - low - ing straight the No - el star?
In - to this sta - ble poor and drear?"

Birds from the woods in won - drous flight,
"Has - t'ning we seek the new - born King,

Beth - le - hem seek this Ho - ly Night.
And all our sweet - est mu - sic bring."

3. Angels and shepherds, birds of the sky,
Come where the Son of God doth lie;
Christ on the earth with man doth dwell,
Join in the shout, Noel, Noel!

I Saw Three Ships

ENGLISH CAROL

Many Christmas customs, such as
yule logs and plum puddings,
have come to us from England.

Joyfully

Three ships sail - ing, three ships sail - ing;

Three ships sail - ing, sail - ing,

1. I saw three ships come sail - ing in, On Chris - si - mas Day,

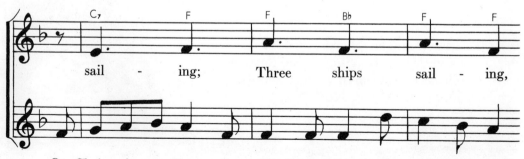

sail - ing; Three ships sail - ing,

On Chris - si - mas Day, I saw three ships come sail - ing in,

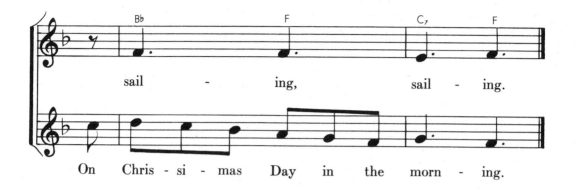

sail - ing, sail - ing.

On Chris - si - mas Day in the morn - ing.

2. And what was in those ships all three,
   On Chrissimas Day, on Chrissimas Day?
   And what was in those ships all three,
   On Chrissimas Day in the morning?

3. The Wise Men three were in those ships,
   On Chrissimas Day, on Chrissimas Day.
   The Wise Men three were in those ships,
   On Chrissimas Day in the morning.

Christmas Greeting

Learn the melody very well before
you sing this song as a round.

TRADITIONAL ROUND

God bless all good friends here, A mer - ry,

mer - ry Christ- mas And a hap - py New Year.

All Glory, Laud, and Honor

TRANS. BY JOHN M. NEALE
MUSIC BY MELCHIOR TESCHNER

Steadily

1. All glo - ry, laud, and hon - or To Thee, Re - deem - er, King,
2. The com - pa - ny of an - gels Are prais - ing Thee on high,

To whom the lips of chil - dren Made sweet ho - san - nas ring.
And mor - tal men and all things Cre - a - ted make re - ply.

Thou art the King of Is - ra - el, Thou Da - vid's roy - al Son,
The peo - ple of the He - brews, With palms be - fore Thee went;

Who in the Lord's name com - est, The King and bless - ed One.
Our praise and prayer and an - thems Be - fore Thee we pre - sent.

Easter Hymn

WORDS BY CHRISTOPHER WORDSWORTH
MUSIC BY VAN DENMAN THOMPSON

Majestically

1. Al - le - lu - ia! Al - le - lu - ia! Hearts to
2. Al - le - lu - ia! Al - le - lu - ia! Glo - ry

heaven and voic - es raise; Sing to God a hymn of
be to God on high; Al - le - lu - ia to the

glad - ness, Sing to God a hymn of praise:
Sav - ior Who has won the vic - to - ry;

Christ has tri - umphed, and we con - quer by His
Al - le - lu - ia to the Spir - it, Fount of

might - y en - ter - prise; We with Him to life e -
love and sanc - ti - ty; Al - le - lu - ia! Al - le -

ter - nal By His res - ur - rec - tion rise. ___
lu - ia! To the Ho - ly Trin - i - ty. ___

183

From Maine to California

WORDS BY MADELEINE A. DUFAY
FRENCH FOLK TUNE

From Maine to sun - ny Cal - i - for - nia, Where our
From Wash - ing - ton right down to Geor - gia, When we

flag is fly - ing high, Wav - ing proud - ly 'cross the sky,

see the flag ap - pear, We give a cheer! __ The stars and

stripes lead on to glo - ry, __ wher - ev - er men love

lib - er - ty, __ It tells the world our na - tion's sto - ry

From Ha - wai - i to A - las - ka see Old Glo - ry fly - ing free.

Classified Index

Song Titles

Listening Themes